The History of Indentureship and South Asian Slavery

Sibani Roy

Published by New Generation Publishing in 2025

Copyright © Sibani Roy 2025

First Edition

ISBN 978-1-83563-608-4

www.newgeneration-publishing.com

New Generation Publishing

ABOUT THE AUTHOR

Dr Sibani Roy, a former Mayor of Colwyn Bay, is an Ethicist also a Fellow for life at the Institute of Hospitality. She is originally from Calcutta, currently known as Kolkata. Now she has made North Wales (UK) her home, a happy home away from home, where she came as an international student, fell in love with the place and people. Sibani has not been a victim of racism herself, but many of her friends did. Therefore, with kind support of her local MP, she founded The North Wales Association of Multicultural Integration, which now is known as The Network for World's Awareness of Multicultural Integration. Her great regret is that coming from Calcutta, she knew nothing about South Asian Indentureship when thousands of people were recruited as indenture labour and shipped from Calcutta port to sugar plantation fields of British colonial countries. She is now determined to learn and tell the people the history of South Asian Indentureship, a dark side of British Indian administration.

This book is dedicated to all Indentured
labours and their descendants

ACKNOWLEDGMENT

I sincerely acknowledge support of

Dr Kumar Mahabir

Salima Mohamed

Dr Dived Dabideen

Oliver Ferrell

Raja Asad

Dr. Radica Mahase

Judith Misrahi-Barak

: Goolam Vahed

Liz Millman

Indo Caribbean Culture entre

Ameena Kapoor Institute for Studies of

Indentureship

And all Interviewees

CONTENTS

FOREWORD

As I write this foreword, I am contemplating the fact that not long ago, in June 2020, none of us could have imagined ourselves living the lives that we lived during the Covid-19 pandemic, and making the changes that we did. The pandemic turned our lives upside down and made us see the world differently.

As an anthropologist, I thrive on meeting people in the field to research their lives in a very personal way. The lockdowns and other restrictions that accompanied the pandemic impacted a large part of my work, and indeed my very life, and the lives of others. To a large degree, we are shaped by the challenges we face in life – the severity of them and how we respond to them personally; how they break us, inform us, reform us, remake us, or even destroy us.

Displacement from one's home is a particularly harrowing challenge. Nowadays, we see a large number of refugees and asylum seekers fleeing the impact of human conflict and climate change in their homelands every year. They are often forced to cope with unimaginable adversities as they strive to survive in a hostile world.

One of the positives of the pandemic was my creation of weekly Indo-Caribbean Cultural Centre (ICC) Zoom public meetings, which have now numbered well over a hundred to date. Through this virtual platform, I came into contact with the author of this book, Dr Sibani Roy, who is now a valued and valuable member of our audience.

Dr Roy is originally from India, but has long resided in North Wales, UK, as an accomplished professional with many strings to her bow. Among other attributes, she is a medical ethicist, a councillor and former mayor of Colwyn Bay, a chaplain of Bangor University, and the founder and chair of Networking for World Awareness of Multicultural Integration (NWAMI). With so many responsibilities to fulfil, she still found time to write this book, adding it to her list of accomplishments and contributions to society.

In this highly readable book, Dr Roy acknowledges the need to place the story of South Asian indentureship into the history of slavery as a whole, by first taking us on a journey through the annals of time, starting with a brief overview of the days of slavery through the ages. The transatlantic slave trade and indentureship originated from the need for cheap labour for the sugar plantations. Dr Roy also enlightens us on the history of that sweet, seductive commodity that has caused – and still causes – so much misery, noting with grim irony that western countries, who could manage very well without sugar, were compelled to be addicted to this slow poison created by their very own people. We pay for our addiction now with exploding rates of obesity and diabetes.

Dr Roy has set herself the task of addressing a wide range of questions on both slavery and indenture: What was the agenda of slavery? What were the customs and norms of different countries and nations towards the concept of slavery? Why did, and when did, slavery really end, and how and why did indentureship begin? Why were South Asians selected to be contracted labourers by the Caribbean and other planter classes? Under what circumstances did Indians agree to sell themselves and their children to the ruthless planters?

Dr Roy offers a thorough documentation of the history of slavery in the New World colonies, from inception to abolition, all of which set the scene for the introduction of the South Asian Indian indentured labourers. She explains that when the British abolished slavery in 1834, and then in 1838 they abandoned the "apprenticeship" system that had followed it, plantation owners were left in need of a substantial supply of cheap labour in order to continue profiting from the sugar trade. They experimented with the importation of workers from Madeira, China, West Africa and India, but eventually settled on Indians as the most suitable substitutes for the enslaved Africans who had previously been at their disposal.

At that time, British-ruled India was rife with British-created famine and other intolerable conditions that made survival untenable for many. Why did Indians opt to leave their homeland? Why would anyone take this drastic step? In the India of the nineteenth and early twentieth centuries, in many cases it was the only feasible choice for survival. As a result of the collapse of industry, a decrease of agriculture, the caste system and taxation, as well as poor wages and the 1857 rebellion, the impoverished sold their own and their children's services. South Indian pariahs (untouchables), *pannaiyals* and *padiyals* (lower castes of agricultural labourers) sold themselves and their children into lifetime debts, because even this was seen as preferable to the oppressions heaped upon them due to their social status.

About one million people signed (and sometimes were forced or tricked into signing) contracts that usually indentured them for between five and ten years, for the journey across the *kalapani*, the "black water", to the sugarcane fields of Mauritius, Fiji, South Africa and the Caribbean. They hoped for an improvement in their fortunes, but were too often met with cruelty, exploitation and deplorable conditions.

Dr Roy relates the history of slavery and indentureship with energy and empathy, drawing us into her narration sometimes with exhaustive detail. And sometimes, it seems, she stands back with us, her readers, to look on in astonishment and indignation at this sad history of suffering and abuse.

When the South Asian indentured labourers chose – or, in many cases, were forced to choose, whether by circumstance or coercion – this unknown and uncertain future, they had no idea in what ways their lives would be changed and affected by the brave act of setting out across the ocean to a strange new world, nor of what kind of life they would bequeath to future generations.

Perhaps for many who have indentured forebears in their family trees, the most moving chapters of the book will be the latter ones, where the descendants of South Asian indentured labourers tell the stories of those who preceded them, and indeed their own stories and perspectives as people whose lives have in many ways been shaped by the events of centuries past. However, it is important to note that these perspectives are not all bleak – we end on a positive note which rightly points out how the entrepreneurial spirit that the indentured must have been imbued with to have even contemplated making their journeys in the first place is what also then led many of them to lead prosperous lives in these new lands once their contracts had concluded.

The Indian diaspora now stretches far and wide, and has managed to flourish in communities all over the world. Yet, the dark origins of Indian emigration from the mother country, when indentured labourers were dispatched to far-flung locations for the enrichment of their rapacious colonial masters – a history filled with filth, ill-treatment, misery, gloom and pain – are, unlike the transatlantic slave trade, little known, and hardly spoken of.

Some historians have dedicated much of their life's work to finding and preserving the histories and legacies of the indentured, highlighting their stories, struggles and achievements (against all the odds), as well as the stories, struggles and achievements of those who have followed in their wake. Therefore, this book is a valuable contribution, and any book about the indentureship of South Asian labourers touches me in a very personal way, because it tells the story of my own ancestral family's struggles. And indeed it is the story of hundreds of thousands of contemporary South Asians – even those who are not yet aware of this.

With such a significant aspect of South Asian diaspora history so thoroughly neglected, it is imperative that this story be broadcast more widely. Dr Roy's book is, therefore, a much-needed addition to the literature on this subject, and I welcome its publication.

Dr Kumar Mahabir
Anthropologist, University of Guyana
Former Assistant Professor, University of Trinidad and Tobago

PhD Anthropology, University of Florida
BA, MPhil., Literatures in English, University of the West Indies, Trinidad and Tobago

INTRODUCTION

Britain was once the most powerful nation on Earth. This relatively small island achieved such status with a widespread colonisation system that reached across a large swath of the world. Political maps of the time indicated British rule in pink, and looking at flat map designs, with Britain in the middle, showed this colour trail stretching from the northwest of Canada, down to and across the Equator, and extending as far as the southeast corner of the globe. Along the way, pink is stamped on much of eastern United States, large chunks of Africa, parts of the Middle East, major landmasses of South Asia (including the entirety of what is now India, Pakistan and Bangladesh), some Southeast Asian nations and the entire Australian continent, taking in myriad islands (most notably in the Caribbean and South Pacific) along the way. The British Empire was the largest the world had ever seen, presiding over every kind of climate, geography and economy, and imposing itself on innumerable cultures, languages and religions. Beginning in the early seventeenth century, the peak of this economic and political power was reached in the early nineteenth century, and it still exists, albeit in a vastly diminished form, today. All told, almost a hundred nations or territories were at one point occupied either in part or in whole by Great Britain. Even today, though its power and reach is greatly reduced, Britain has 17 overseas territories and crown dependencies (admittedly small islands) and its monarch is recognised as the head of state in 15 countries.

Perhaps inevitably, such power, reach and influence could not be achieved and maintained without some nefarious practices. While there are those who, both historically and to this day, champion the Empire and its excesses as the "glory days" of Great Britain, it is undeniable that a great many people suffered under it. The downsides of the Empire are well documented, from its involvement in slavery to the subjugation of countries, cultures and communities, and from its exploitation of natural resources to leaving impoverished former colonial nations to fend for themselves after allowing their independence only once they had ceased to be useful to Britain. Even so, there is at least one lost chapter in this history – a story of the struggle of almost two million people moved around the Empire and to its farthest shores between 1834 and 1920; almost two million people dispatched under false pretences, or whose illiteracy was taken advantage of, who were sold a lie about work, about money, about their prospects and about their final destination – from where most would never return. This was a system called "indentured labour", a more palatable terminology for what was essentially a continuation of the slave trade after the latter was legally abolished in 1833.

Having typically targeted Africa for slaves, the British turned their attentions largely to the Indian subcontinent when the indentureship system was launched. Those unfortunate enough to be lured into it

– well in excess of a million Indians, and tens of thousands more each from several other countries and territories – found themselves bound by contracts many could neither read nor understand, not knowing where they were being taken, what the purpose of their stretching voyage was, nor if they would ever return to their native land. Most of them would not.

It was one of the major movements of people in the nineteenth century, yet it is sophistically ignored in most historical records; its evidence often suppressed even to this day. It is a tale of misery, exploitation, injustice and abuse of power.

While the indentureship of South Asians was a phenomenon of the nineteenth century, the seeds of its practice were sown hundreds of years before, beginning with Christopher Columbus's expedition to the New World in 1492. This voyage led to the first known contact with the Caribbean by Europeans and triggered colonial expansion into the region. This expansion would become firmly linked to the sugar industry, the plantation system and, in turn, the slave trade of black Africans. Europe's connection to the Caribbean – and thus the Caribbean's connection to sugar – has lasted for more than five centuries since. It remains a divisive issue, because while the region has undoubtedly benefitted commercially from the crop, this has led to an economic reliance on it, to say nothing of the vast human rights abuses committed in the course of profiting from it.

The link between black African slaves and sugar plantations in the Caribbean is well known, but the issue of rights abuses in the industry was much more widespread and complex, involving other races of people, particularly South Asians, who found themselves in a very similar position to the African slaves once slavery was legally abolished. Instead, they were mistreated under the more palatable (to European sentimentalities) arrangement known as "indentured labour".

This book aims to raise awareness of the suffering that the South Asian indentured labourers endured, to explain how and why this was allowed to happen, and what led to the implementation of the system. In doing so, there is no attempt made to compare their experience with that of the African slaves, nor to diminish the traumas experienced by the latter, but rather to issue an appeal for the plight of the indentured workers to be similarly recognised, not only for the posthumous sake of those who made these ill-fated voyages from South Asia, but also for the benefit of contemporary societies which continue to feel the ramifications of these events. It also seeks to hold accountable the people who instigated indenture, those who benefited from it despite knowing it was a trade in human misery, and those who have, over the course of history, either justified it or, worse, deliberately ignored or downplayed what was, in practice, little different to slavery and, in legality, no more than a rebranding of a vile system; a loophole ruthlessly exploited so money could continue to be made off the back of the lives of humans.

By delving into the histories that led to indentureship, this book considers its impact, both then and now, on the millions of Indians, Caribbeans and British nationals, as well as people from various other countries and regions that were involved, and how it played a critical role in the evolution of the British Empire and the Caribbean region, and in today's complex nation-building and societal issues.

By gaining a deeper understanding of the issue, and an awareness of the flawed version of this history as propagated by outdated, pro-colonial texts, it is hoped readers will grasp the fundamentals of ruling and being ruled, of colonisers and occupations, actions and consequences, moments and revolutions – the same things which serve as the entire mechanism of the world's functionality, but which in this case has been sorely under-represented.

SLAVERY: ITS HISTORY AND HOW IT IS MISUNDERSTOOD

slavery
[noun]
the activity of legally owning other people who are forced to work for or obey you

The Cambridge Dictionary's definition of slavery is clear, and from this we can make the distinction between it and indenture – and realise that this distinction is but a slight one, and one that indentured workers were largely powerless to do anything about. No, indentured workers were not "owned" – it's just that they couldn't leave. And no, they were not "forced" to work, in that they had signed their contracts – it's just that many of them did not (and often *could* not) know what they were signing up for. Their employers knew this. In all likelihood, that will have been precisely why they were recruited.

Whatever the truth about indentureship, its roots were planted firmly in the slave trade which preceded it. As such, it is important to understand slavery before we can begin to understand indentureship. There are questions we must answer about slavery, its history, its impact and legacy, its current-day application, and the similarities and differences between it and indenture.

The most important misconceptions to clarify about slavery are the two which are most persistent in contemporary culture and thinking: that it was something that primarily affected black Africans and their descendants, and that it is a practice that has been long confined to history. Neither is true. Slavery dates back many centuries, has been practised by, and endured by, every major race, and still happens in some places today (albeit illegally). Even where it has long been outlawed, its effects continue to be felt.

The custom of slavery was historically prevalent in almost every civilisation, including the Roman and other European empires. The Dutch were among the first of the European maritime nations to become involved in the transatlantic slave trade, carrying approximately half a million Africans across the ocean between 1596 and 1829. A large number of these people were transported to the Caribbean colonies of Dutch Guiana (now Suriname), Curaçao and Sint Eustatius, though the majority were trans-shipped to America and the Spanish territories. So, while these two islands did take on a number of slaves, they also served as staging areas for the resale and onward shipment of Africans who had survived their voyage along their part of the Middle Passage, the name given to the triangular shipping route which began in Europe, visited Africa to pick up slaves, moved across the Atlantic to sell them, and then returned to Europe carrying the cargo purchased with the proceeds of the sales of humans. The Dutch found, however, that slave labour wasn't especially profitable, though they clung to the belief it would pay off in the long run. They stubbornly continued with it until 1863, making it one of the last European countries to abolish slavery. With this, some 33,000 slaves – estimated to be almost 10 per cent of its population at the time – were emancipated in what is now Suriname, and another 12,000 in other Dutch colonies.

Slavery had existed in the French colonies since the early sixteenth century, and by 1778 France was bringing in some 13,000 African slaves to its West Indies territories each year. The trade was outlawed in 1794 by the National Convention, the legislature which followed the abolition of the French monarchy two years prior. The National Convention would only last for three years, though these were three highly eventful and controversial years, characterised by rebellion, division, economic failures and the civil war which erupted following the execution of King Louis XVI in 1793. Still, its legacy was undeniable: France has been a republic ever since, and its ban on slavery has largely remained in place (notwithstanding Napoleon restarting the trade in 1802 and then reversing his decision 13 years later – though official abolition, for the last time, did not come into effect until 1848).

All told, Europeans – most notably the British, French, Dutch, Spanish and Portuguese – ruled over much of the globe for hundreds of years, establishing colonies on all continents, as well as enslaving a diverse group of people from every major race, religion, race and culture.

Meanwhile, over the course of centuries of war in the Mediterranean, both Muslims and Christians would typically enslave one another after conquering them in battle. Western and Central Asians, Indians and Eastern and Northern Africans were the most commonly enslaved peoples during this time. The Arabs found West Asia, North Africa and Southeast Africa to be hotbeds for procuring slave labour. The Ottoman Empire exploited humans from the Caucasus, Eastern and Central Europe, Western Asia and Northern Africa for much of its 600-year history, which began in the late fourteenth century. And traffickers from the Barbary Coast targeted North Africa, the Mediterranean and even the British Isles and Iceland between the 16th and nineteenth centuries.

It was not until after World War I that the process of repressing slavery began in Muslim states, primarily owing to pressure from Western governments, such as Britain and France, though outright abolition did not occur until some time later. The Ottoman Empire banned slavery in 1924, a year after the new Turkish Constitution dissolved the Imperial Harem and made its remaining concubines and eunuchs free citizens of the newly declared Republic of Turkey. Five years later, Iran abolished slavery. It wasn't until 1962 that Saudi Arabia and Yemen followed suit, and 1970 for Oman.

Even they, though, were well ahead of Mauritania, which was the last country in the world to outlaw slavery, and which essentially still accepts it today. Mauritania has actually banned slavery (on paper) twice: first, it was attempted by the French colonial government of the time in 1905, though this proved unenforceable and was rescinded upon independence in 1960. A presidential decree then abolished the slave trade as late as 1981, though stopped short of criminalising the practice. This meant it largely continued. It wasn't until 2007 that the Mauritanian government bowed to international pressure and decreed that slaveholders could be prosecuted. In reality, though, such prosecutions are next-to non-existent, with only one known example – a six-month prison term handed to Oumoulmoumnine Mint Bakar Vall in 2011 for enslaving two girls, aged ten and 14, as maids. Those six months were the same length of imprisonment handed to three human rights activists who dared to protest against slavery at the same time of the trial in the Mauritanian capital, Nouakchott.

Despite government insistence to the contrary, reports suggest slavery continues to be largely tolerated in Mauritania even now. In 2017, the BBC claimed some 600,000 people in the country were in bonded labour, and a year later the Global Slavery Index reported an estimate of 90,000 slaves living there. If true, that represents almost 2 per cent of the country's population – or, in other words, one in 50 people living in Mauritania is a slave. That doesn't include the vastly bigger number of reported bonded labourers – or those working under the indenture system, to give it its more palatable terminology, which was used to justify the exploitation of Indians by Britain in the nineteenth century.

But the abolishment of slavery in other countries similarly did not always put an end to the practice, especially in Britain. It was simply "rebranded" as indenture, the target moved from Africa to South Asia, and then the trade in human cargo continued, much as it did before, so that British planters could continue to be served. So, we should be under no illusion that slavery was experienced exclusively by black Africans, or that it was a trade with a limited or specific timeframe in history.

The sugar industry was thriving magnificently in the early nineteenth century, and this hungry machinery required an enormous workforce to function optimally. So, the Empire's Slavery Abolition Act of 1833 left British planters in the Caribbean facing the prospect of having to maintain massive sugar production levels, but to do so without the free labour to which they had become accustomed. The answer, while staying within the confines of the law, was indentured labour, approved by the British government five years after its ban on slavery, which allowed recruiters to essentially trick people into willingly signing up to work on the plantations, by offering what on paper seemed to be a valid contract of employment, but which in reality was little different to slavery. To take advantage of this loophole, planters targeted the poor and the illiterate; people with no prospects who could be tempted by the prospect of even a meagre payday to go and work abroad, and who could often not even read what they were signing up for – a life of hard labour in a faraway land for precious little recompense and little or no chance of ever going back home. It was one of history's grossest violations of human rights, engulfing the lives of more than a million men, women and children from the Indian subcontinent, and yet this – and they – have barely been mentioned subsequently.

Life on the plantations

As a result of the inflow of enslaved Africans into the New World, acts for "controlling the negroes" were created. Slave laws drawn up by island legislatures reveal a lot about how enslaved Africans were treated and how slavery was practised in the Caribbean colonies. These laws established legal norms, but they were designed not to protect the safety and rights of the workers; rather, they aimed to safeguard planters against the prospect of insurrection.

To crush opposition and "domesticate" the enslaved Africans, the planters used an array of cruel tactics which would have previously been unlawful, but which were now permitted under landowners' civil rules and codes which were authorised for the corporal punishment of slaves found guilty of crimes, or at least of crimes as defined by such lopsided regulations.

Under these laws, if tried and found guilty of acts such as stealing or destroying property, the slave was to be publicly lashed. If the slave committed the same act again, they could have their noses slit and their foreheads branded with a hot iron. A third conviction could lead to the death penalty. At the same time, if a slave owner maimed or killed a slave while beating the victim overzealously, there would be no repercussions.

Planters were required to keep slave cabins under tight supervision, and slaves were forbidden to possess any kind of firearms or armaments. Any mutiny, insurgency or revolt that did crop up was dealt with even more severely than the prescribed punishments for theft or vandalism, while attempts to escape could result in a returned slave being fitted with an iron yoke to prevent any further flights for freedom.

The purpose of such regulations was to instil in the slaves a fear that the consequences of attempts to escape or rebel would be even worse than the dire fate they were already enduring.

Women's and children's roles

Historically, women were considered fragile and inadequate for manual labour – although this was not the case for the women working on sugar plantations in the West Indies.

Enslaved women worked shoulder to shoulder with men. In such critical environments, with unsanitary practices, malnutrition and backbreaking work, many women lost their ability to conceive. This was to the advantage of the planters, who had to take on the costs of raising any children born to slaves. It was much easier to buy an African adult than to have to wait for a child to reach working age, paying for their upkeep along the way.

This explains why enslaved women in the Caribbean had, comparatively, a very small number of children, and many of the children they did have died at a very young age. It's written in the diaries of a Jamaican planter, Thomas Thistlewood, that 153 pregnancies were recorded over a period of 37 years at his plantation. Thirty two of these ended in miscarriage, and of the 121 live births, 51 of those children died before the age of seven. That makes a ratio of fewer than one in three pregnancies resulting in a child surviving to seven years of age.

Jennifer L Morgan, Professor of Social and Cultural Analysis and History at New York University, wrote that the routine loss of children was one of the hidden traumas of slavery. In these circumstances, we can assume that for many enslaved women, their pregnancy experience was one of pain and poor health, and then often one of grief. And even if a baby survived, their childhood would be one of neglected physical and emotional needs.

The causes of these high rates of miscarriage and child mortality are still being discussed, but it is evident that the work environment the women operated in, which required extremely intense physical activity in conditions of poor nutrition, had a significant impact. The vast bulk of this activity was agricultural. Enslaved women were mostly engaged in harsh manual labour, producing commercial crops, most notably sugar, the estates for which housed more than 60 per cent of all enslaved persons in the Caribbean.

African children were unwitting participants in the slave trade, too. As well as those born into the trade, there were others who were uprooted from their homes, just as the adults were. Sometimes they were bought and sold, while others were kidnapped. This was particularly so in West Africa, from where slavers would snatch them while they worked (legitimately) in fields, wandered around towns on their own, or even just played outside.

They were particularly vulnerable in war zones, where the majority of able-bodied men had left their communities to go and fight, and often to die. These massively reduced adult male populations left women, children and the elderly ripe for the picking, as prisoners of war, to be torn from their homes and put to work abroad.

Even the soldiers were not safe from being trafficked. With demand for slave labour growing exponentially in the eighteenth century, traders had to find more and more ways to maintain the supply of workers. Whereas before they had focused on coastal communities, because of ease of transporting this human cargo to their ships, they would now push further inland. Mercenary expeditions into Africa were regularly accompanied by commercial caravans, who would trade textiles and other commodities for captured soldiers.

Children in particular were valued, because adult slaves had an average useful working life of just five to seven years. This working life was often curtailed by death, which again was preferable to the planters, as it meant they would not have to spend on the upkeep of any slaves who were still alive but no longer physically capable of working. Employing child slaves meant there was a chance of a greater return on investment in terms of working lifespan.

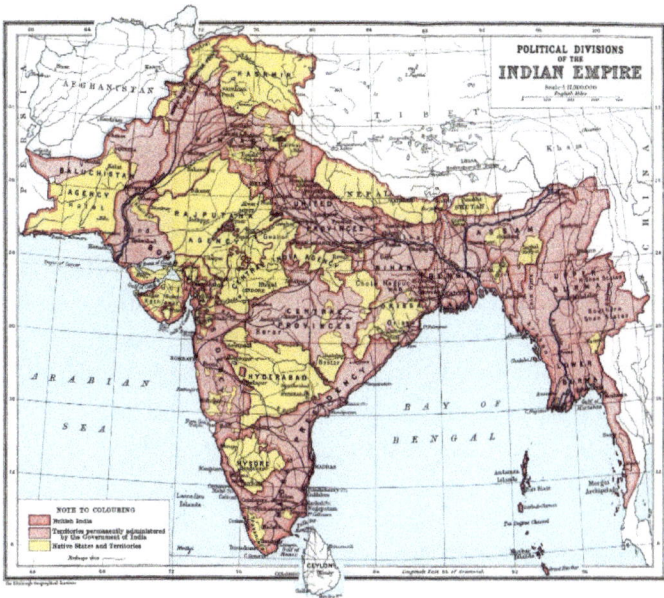

SUGAR: ITS BITTERSWEET ROLE IN HUMAN MISERY

Sugar abounds in the food and drink of modern society. It is found, often in high quantities, in many of the things we drink and eat. Its over-consumption by individuals is blamed for various health maladies, from dental cavities and obesity to heart disease and diabetes. Some people may even develop a sugar addiction. And yet it is presented as, and viewed as, an innocent product. While Americans consume as much as 100lb of sugar per person per year – some 60lbs of which is considered "added sugar" (that is, an ingredient which is not naturally present in the product), precious few of them consider what that soda, or candy, or chocolate bar, or milkshake is doing to their body. Fewer still will spare a thought for the millions of people who suffered in one of history's darkest periods, as Europeans pursued the huge profits from this crop they would term "white gold".

Sugar's value was largely due to its flavour, and later as the base for distilling rum, but it had other uses. It has preservative properties, helping a food to keep its taste, texture and colour, as well as remaining safe to eat for longer. This explains the high levels of it which can be found in some tropical foodstuffs, such as curries. It also prevents the growth of micro-organisms, helping to prolong the shelf life of canned foods.

Going back as far as ancient Greece and Rome, sugar was primarily used as a medication, and these properties were touted along with its culinary uses when sugar was brought to England in the twelfth century via the fabled Silk Road trade routes across the Middle East. It was purported to cure anything from fevers and coughs to chapped lips, chest problems and stomach disorders, although it was only available to the rich, sold as it was as a spice, typically mixed with ginger, saffron or cinnamon.

Today, sugar is not really thought of as a medicine, but is of course still a very common (too common?) ingredient in food and is prized as a renewable agricultural raw material with applications in energy generation, fermentation and sucrochemical industries. It is still among the world's five most valuable soft commodities in terms of yearly consumption, alongside cocoa, coffee, wheat and cotton.

Sugar's roots as a commercial crop can be traced all the way back to about 8,000BC, when the people of New Guinea in Melanesia took sugarcane with them as they migrated first to several South Pacific islands, and later to Indonesia, the Philippines and India. Gradually, it reached Arabia, where several countries were found to have ideal climates for the crop. By the sixteenth century, it was well established as a major industry in the region, as the Arabs improved the technique of refining sugar in mills, allowing the trade to expand. At the time, the Arab nations had an excess of sugar and the region's wealthy people were major consumers, but it remained prohibitively expensive for most foreign markets and was in low supply in other parts of the world.

Sugar's presence in Europe, and in turn the Americas, can also be traced to the Arabs, and their occupation of large parts of Portugal between 711 and 1294. The crop could grow in the warmer climes of this Southern European nation and it continued to be cultivated by independent Portugal. After Portugal itself became a colonial power, it took sugar to Brazil when it arrived in the South American country in 1500. This came not long after Christopher Columbus had introduced sugar to Hispaniola, when he carried the crop there from the Canary Islands during his second voyage to the New World.

Brazil proved to be an excellent location for cultivating sugar, and Portugal found this an ideal place from where to keep up with the enormous and increasing demand for the crop. Inevitably, this required the widespread employment of slaves, and it is estimated that by 1550, 38.3 per cent of Rio de Janeiro's population was made up of them. Even more slaves passed through Rio as cargo as the city became one of the world's main ports receiving African slave ships. Brazil today is the world's leading producer of sugar, which perfectly illustrated the impact the trade had on the entire Americas, a continent on which the crop had never naturally grown before.

Although the Portuguese Empire initially controlled the sugar trade in the Americas, the Dutch–Portuguese War would result in a change that would have ramifications for the sugar business in the Caribbean, notably rum manufacturing (made from sugar cane juice). In 1630, the Dutch captured Recife in

Pernambuco, in what is now Brazil (the Dutch dubbed it New Holland when they assumed control), including its sugar plantations operated by African slaves who had been brought to the region by the Portuguese.

By the mid seventeenth century, the Dutch were heavily involved in slavery, though the Netherlands did not manufacture sugar in the Caribbean, as the necessary land conditions were not widespread in its territories there. Instead, as well as Brazil, its South American colony Dutch Guiana (now Suriname) was preferred, and the Netherlands employed slaves there in much the same way as its European counterparts did in the Caribbean. The Dutch found, however, that slave labour wasn't especially profitable, though they clung to the belief it would pay off in the long run. They stubbornly continued with it until 1863, making it one of the last European countries to abolish it.

Meanwhile, other parts of South and Central America were being identified by the colonial powers as viable locations for sugar farming, and this would later spread to what is now the United States.

English planters began growing sugarcane in Barbados in the 1640s, staffed by a mixture of convicts from the British Isles and enslaved people from Africa. A plantocracy civilisation quickly developed there because of the great demand for sugar.

Cuba, did, however have excellent conditions for sugar cultivation and, sure enough, slavery followed, as part of Spain's involvement in the trade. However, despite the country prospering commercially from the crop, its populace were not big supporters of slavery and largely ceased partaking in it in 1867, followed by official abolishment in 1886. This made Cuba one of the earliest colonies to outlaw slavery, aided by a strong independence movement that would lead to separation from Spain by the early twentieth century.

France, too, was a major player in the slave trade in the late eighteenth century, behind only the Portuguese and British in terms of numbers of individuals it bought and sold, mostly taken from Africa to St Domingue (Haiti, as it was known when a French colony), but its method was different. The French Republic was also capitalising on the demand for sugar, but did not use slaves to work the fields, because land in France and its colonies was not well suited to the crop. Instead, the French practised what was known as the 'circuit trade', in which ships filled with commercial goods travelled to Africa, where the commodities were swapped for slaves. These slaves were then swapped in the Caribbean for sugar and other goods to be sold back in Europe. Enslaved Africans were viewed as nothing more than goods in the trading system in which France was participating.

Sugar agriculture was very profitable and quickly spread throughout the Caribbean and to Louisiana and Mississippi in North America. By the mid nineteenth century, more than ten million Africans had been forcefully transported to the New World and divided across the sugar fields of the Americas so that Europeans could enjoy sugar and rum, the main products of the crop. A third of Europe's economy depended on sugar by this time and it was by far the most significant foreign commodity. By diversifying plantation outputs and improving efficiency, sugar barons from St Kitts to Jamaica became extraordinarily wealthy.

The United States, though, was possibly the most notorious slave trader of them all, especially due to it importing vast numbers to work – and to be bought and sold – within its own country rather than in overseas territories. The environment of certain parts of the US, particularly in the south, lent itself well to sugar production, as well as several other crops, most notably cotton and tobacco, and America's position today as an economic colossus can be largely attributed to its widespread abuse of humans.

How rum furthered the thirst for sugar

Although there are historical tales of rum-like beverages in the Far East, the drink we know today as rum developed as a byproduct of the sugar trade in the colonial West Indies. Those labouring on sugar plantations in the seventeenth century discovered that fermenting and distilling molasses created alcohol, and so modern rum was created.

Other areas of the world developed their own fermented sugar-based beverages independently of the Caribbean, but Caribbean rum came to dominate, mostly due to its position in the seventeenth-century global economy dominated by colonial European powers. Production of this Caribbean style of rum was then expanded across the colonies, where locations offered suitable conditions, and it could soon be found in parts of North America, India and Australia, among others.

It proved so popular that it became a drink of both legend and infamy. It had a strong maritime association, with sailors in the British Royal Navy receiving a daily ration of it as part of their pay package until as recently as 1970. And, most famously, Admiral

Nelson's body was quickly immersed in a barrel of rum following his death in the Battle of Trafalgar in 1805, so it may be preserved for his journey home from Spain to England.

Meanwhile, the first President of the United States, George Washington, ordered a barrel of Barbadian rum to be served at the celebration dinner marking his inauguration in 1789, having grown fond of the drink during time spent in Barbados as a young man.

Even fonder still of rum were the Australians, who staged a military coup in New South Wales when the state governor, William Bligh, reportedly sought to limit its use as a de facto currency by outlawing the bartering of rum and introducing government control of ships in port, many of which were bringing the drink into the country from India. This attempt to disrupt what was essentially a monopoly run by the New South Wales Corps triggered what would be Australia's first and so far only armed ouster of a government.

In a horrible chain known as the Triangular Trade, rum was also used as a currency with which to buy African slaves – slaves who would help farm the sugar that would make the rum which would then be transported back to Africa and used to buy more slaves. By the late seventeenth century, Caribbean rum was highly prized and a booming export. African tribal chiefs would gladly accept barrels of rum from colonial traders in return for the lives of their very own people, of whom an estimated 30 per cent would perish during their voyage to the Americas. Slaves in transit being sold in other ports in Europe and elsewhere could also often be purchased with rum. This practice continued for many years. According to British traders, there was no trade to be had without rum in Sierra Leone by 1725.

Initially, rum was a rather harsh drink, and certainly an exceptionally strong one. One of the very few "perks" the slaves enjoyed was an allocation of rum, though this was more likely distributed to them as a soporific, so they would be subdued after their long hours of hard labour and not be vulnerable to thoughts of rebellion.

The quality of rum did improve, though, in line with the increase in its popularity around the world. This led the British to ban the importation of foreign rum in 1764, to protect its indigenous spirits. The French enacted similar laws for similar reasons in the 1790s.

Molasses was then brought to the new American colonies and distilled, establishing America's first commercially manufactured alcohol, and creating a demand for rum that exists to this day in the United States.

Its popularity there fell over the nineteenth century, though, as a result of limits on sugar imports and the emergence of American whiskey. At the same time, the Caribbean sugar industry began to dwindle as first Napoleon instigated in 1811 that sugar be produced from beet (while statistically sugar cane offers a higher yield than beet, sugar beet lends itself to a faster production times and can be grown in a wider variety of climates than cane, which is best suited to the tropics), and then in the latter part of the century the colonial powers began to abolish slavery.

The process

Sugar cane was an unusual plant to cultivate, especially for Europeans who were accustomed to producing crops such as wheat, which they would harvest and then send to others to mill into flour. Consequently, European planters in the Americas adopted a largely hands-off approach when it came to production – especially since they had free labour to do the hard work for them.

Slaves essentially performed every physical task on the plantations. They seeded, tended to and then harvested the crop, after which they extracted the juice from the sugar cane, boiled and processed it to convert it into sugar and molasses, and finally extract even the waste products so that this could be used to produce rum. Enslaved men, women and children worked long days all year round on the sugar plantations, which were both farms and factories.

Paintings and drawings from this time made an effort to present life on the sugar plantations as pleasant, with labourers smiling as they worked away outdoors under the blue skies of tropical idylls. However, we must keep in mind that the artists who created these images were attempting to make things look more appealing; they were essentially creating propaganda pieces aimed at defending slavery and attempting to persuade the public back in Britain that it wasn't so horrible. It is important we don't take these pictures at face value. For sure, the Caribbean islands are beautiful and offer a pleasant climate, but that would have been irrelevant to the slaves as they endured unrelenting hard labour and myriad human rights abuses.

When it came to recruiting for such physical work, for the planters it was a case of the younger, the better. Whether the slaves had been bought, or had been born and raised on plantations as the children of slaves, young men and women were typically put to hard labour as part of the First Gang as soon as they were strong enough, typically in their mid to late teens. The First Gang performed the hardest tasks, such as digging, hacking the thick canes from near the base, and anything that required heavy lifting or long hours of bending or stooping.

Cane-holing, in particular, was exhausting. First Gang slaves marked out squares of four to six feet, and then dug out that square to a depth of six to nine inches. This was made even more difficult by the fact they were given hoes rather than spades for this task. Each slave would dig out as many as 100 of these squares (depending on their width) every day, which meant excavating up to 1,500 cubic feet of soil, and this soil was then used to build banks around each square. Two young sugar cane plants would be planted inside each hole.

A First Gang member would work from sunrise to sunset, every day. This routine did not lend itself to longevity and these young people would usually be physically debilitated after just ten or twelve years, at which point they would be demoted to the Second Gang – often before they were even 30.

The Second Gang still worked hard, and for long hours, just their tasks were not quite so backbreaking. Their responsibilities included planting seeds, tying the cut canes into bundles, and lighter lifting such as loading bundles on to wagons.

One particularly loathsome task handed to the Second Gang (and some First Gang members) was the transportation of manure. Slaves carried large baskets of animal faeces on their heads to the squares where the young canes had been planted. Each basket was huge, weighing up to 80lb, but this load was only enough to fertilise two squares, or four plants. One acre of sugar cane required up to 1.25 tonnes of dung. Slaves particularly despised this duty, as not only was it physically arduous, it was also filthy.

As well as those former First Gang members who were no longer as fit and strong as they once were, the Second Gang also employed younger teenagers and physically weaker or less-abled slaves. Even the poorly were not granted sick leave – if a First Gang member fell ill but was judged to still be able to work, they would be assigned Second Gang duties until they regained their strength.

Life in the Second Gang would last for about 20 years, before a slave would be moved to the Third Gang. Usually still in their 40s, they were considered old and worn out. Also known as the Grass Gang, this corps would perform the lightest tasks, such as weeding the fields, harvesting animal feed, and vermin control.

Weeding was an unrelenting task, as weeds grow quickly in the tropics and, if left unchecked, can overwhelm crops. The Third Gang had to keep on top of this all year round. They were also tasked with keeping pests at bay, particularly rats, which enjoyed eating immature sugar cane and could number in their thousands on any given plantation. Workers would chase away any that they saw or, even better, set traps for them. This was a rare task which could lead to reward, as some planters offered incentives to slaves who killed the most rodents – usually extra rum.

These older slaves were also joined in the Third Gang by children, who were given such duties as they prepared for the harder work ahead, or by any Second Gang members who were temporarily ruled incapable of performing their duties, such as through sickness or injury. For the slaves who had gone through the Gang system from the start, there would be no formal retirement to look forward to; they simply continued to work in the Third Gang until they no longer could.

Perhaps the best a slave could hope for would be a promotion to the rank of "driver". Slave drivers were drawn from the ranks of labourers, typically experienced older males who had forged a reputation for diligence and obedience. Their responsibility was to supervise crop production and maintain discipline, with the use of violence or threat of violence at their disposal, including whips. While it was surely unpalatable for these drivers to physically punish and verbally scold the lower ranks from which they themselves had come, it was still preferable to hard labour. Besides, they too were managed by white owners and overseers, who expected the drivers to keep the labourers in line and output high, and who could also employ harsh physical punishments for falling short of this. Empathy for fellow slaves was not something that drivers placed a great deal of stock in.

By the time the crop was ready for harvest, usually in February or March, the plants were often taller than a human. Humans, of course, chopped them down, using curved knives known as billhooks, and then stripped the leaves from the canes with the same tool. The canes had to be processed quickly, before the juice inside degraded. Therefore, the First and Second Gangs worked even harder during the harvesting season, first cutting down the crop and then bundling it to the sugar mills and boiling houses, which on larger plantations would run for 24 hours a day, every day except Sunday (even slave owners liked to maintain a façade of Christianity). To maintain this non-stop production, the gangs worked in two twelve-hour shifts – one through the day and one through the night.

The mills were powered by wind, animals or, as you might expect, humans. Slaves fed the canes into rollers, which crushed the plants and squeezed their juice out into pans, which fed the liquid via pipes into the neighbouring boiling houses, first into a storage tank and into a large copper vat or bowl heated by fire underneath. As it boiled, skilled workers stirred the juice and skimmed any solids from the surface. An experienced slave, named the boiler, would determine when the liquid had been sufficiently cleaned and reduced to its desired consistency, so that it would be ladled into a smaller vat, where the process would be repeated. This would happen four or five times, the mixture getting thicker and darker each time. Once the juice was in the final vat, the boiler would pay close attention for signs the mixture was about to crystallise, at which point they would temper it with lime juice before transferring it to a cooling vat. Once sufficiently cooled, the mixture would be transferred to clay pots, in which it would sit for a few days before molasses was drained from the pots through holes in the bottom. The molasses was taken to a still to be turned into rum, while the semi-refined sugar left in the pots was sun-dried, packaged and then shipped to overseas markets, particularly Europe and the wider United States. One gallon of cane juice would produce about a pound of muscovado (semi-refined brown) sugar.

These arduous twelve-hour shifts, and particularly the night shifts, often left the slaves fatigued and sleepy, and a momentary lapse of concentration could have dire consequences. If a worker failed to let go of a sugar cane quickly enough as they fed them into the rollers, they risked having their arms pulled in and crushed. If this happened, they would not be afforded hospital treatment and rehabilitation; rather, any maimed arms would be unceremoniously chopped off with an axe.

There was environmental harm caused by the sugar production process, too. As the business expanded across the Caribbean, negative environmental effects started to manifest. Examples of this included forest degradation, soil erosion, contamination of water supplies and the loss of fertility in arable land. These effects were identified in Santo Domingo (now the Dominican Republic) as early as the sixteenth century and in the Lesser Antilles in the seventeenth century. By the eighteenth century, they could also be seen in St Domingue (now Haiti), and in Cuba and Puerto Rico by the nineteenth century.

Professor Reinaldo Funes Monzote, a Caribbean and Latin American environmental historian based at the University of Havana, wrote in 2018 of the "serious deterioration" of these lands, and of the dire socio-economic repercussions on these communities caused by sugar.

These countries made – and continue to make – efforts to reduce the effects of the sugar production industry, but with their geographies still struggling to physically recover and their people continuing to feel the effects of centuries of abuses, to a large extent the damage has already been done.

EMANCIPATION: CRY FREEDOM (SORT OF)

If you're in the business of making and selling products and you don't have to pay for labour, you can get extremely wealthy very rapidly. That is why generations of white Europeans and Americans loved to employ black Africans as slave labour.

Undoubtedly, the British Empire was thriving by leaps and bounds by the late eighteenth century, and its territories in the Caribbean and the Americas, which were the starting point for the British wholeheartedly embracing the slave trade, were major contributors to this economic success. Sugar, cotton, coffee and tea were the staple products which formed the backbone of the economic growth of the British planter class. The 1700s were the golden years for the planter class, not just for Britain but for all colonial nations. The planters could run their businesses however they chose and treat their slaves in whatever manner they wanted. Slaves were considered little more than livestock, and in some ways were treated even worse than beasts of burden. No limitations were placed on the punishments which could be meted out to them, no checks and balances existed to oversee how plantations were run (so long as they were profitable), and human rights barely merited consideration.

But change was looming, as anti-slavery sentiment had started to brew. Awareness was rising among liberals in Britain as to the true nature of the slave trade and the abuses endured by the slaves, and among the slaves themselves a greater understanding of their rights was growing.

British abolitionists began to fight against the transatlantic trade of African people from around the 1770s onwards, building momentum exponentially. Aiding the abolitionists' cause was a see-sawing British economy and discontent raised by international merchants against British monopolies in Caribbean colonies, as well as the example set by France.

After the French monarchy was brought down in 1792, taking with it slavery two years later, significant slave revolts followed in the British West Indies. France's abolition of slavery included its territories, such as St Domingue, which served as a popular model, since emancipation not only freed the colony's slaves but also led – via former slave-engendered insurrection – to the country's independence, creating in 1804 the world's first black republic, Haiti.

Meanwhile, rising calls for free trade saw other major plantation-based economies, such as those in Brazil and Cuba in particular, become more competitive, and the British struggled to keep up. Consequently, in 1807, Britain and its empire abolished the transatlantic slave trade – though it did not outlaw the use of slavery itself.

The period following the ban on the transatlantic trade was a groundbreaking one, though, which would ultimately prove the catalyst for slave emancipation across the Caribbean as other colonial powers followed suit (although it would still be decades more before the

United States fell in line). Encouraged by the example set by Haiti, significant slave revolts followed in the British Caribbean, most notably Bussa's Rebellion in Barbados in 1816, the Demerara Rebellion in British Guiana in 1823 and the Christmas Uprising, led by Samuel Sharpe in Jamaica over the festive season of 1831-32. While the Barbadian and Guianese insurrections were put down swiftly, the Jamaican revolt proved particularly instrumental in the eventual decision by the British government to end slavery.

Britain's initial ban on the slave trade – though not on slavery itself – introduced several regulations on the sector. For example, owners had to register every slave so that births and deaths could be properly recorded. Limits were also placed on what punishments could be imposed on workers. Such new rules were offensive to many in the planter class, who objected to being dictated to by a government that sat thousands of miles away across an ocean. Of course, the reality was that they were worried by what was the start of the decline of their self-operated kingdom. They were upset that they would no longer be allowed to act with impunity, and they feared that curbs placed on punishments at a time of growing discontent among slaves could increase the risk of rebellion.

There would be no let-up in the pressure from abolitionists for an outright ban. Men and women from all walks of life began to join the cause, especially as a number of public figures did so too, bringing further glare upon the wrongs of slavery. Among the prominent names who got involved in the efforts were the likes of politician William Wilberforce, writer Thomas Clarkson, poet William Cowper, scholar/musician Granville Sharp, surgeon Alexander

Falconbridge, philanthropist Elizabeth Heyrick, Haitian general Toussaint Louverture, ex-slaves Olaudah Equiano and Mary Prince, and John Newton, a former investor in slavery and slave ship captain who changed his ways after witnessing the horrors of the trade and later became an abolitionist. Several abolitionist petitions launched in 1833 alone attracted the signatures of a combined 1.3 million people – an astonishing figure at a time when the population of England and Wales stood at less than 14 million.

The British government could resist this pressure no longer and finally passed the Slavery Abolition Act on August 1 of the following year, putting an (official) end once and for all to the country's role in this vile practice and freeing more than 800,000 slaves across the Empire – some 665,000 of whom were in the Caribbean. In addition to the existing ban on the transatlantic slave trade, the Act further outlawed any purchase, sale or ownership of humans in all of Britain's colonies.

As expected, this was met with strong opposition from the planter class, who had for generations enjoyed a privileged life thanks to their exploitation of fellow humans, and they still commanded enough influence that the government felt it must appease their grievances. To help with this "transition" period, the new law allowed owners to retain their slaves in apprentice roles for a period of four to six years, although children under the age of six were immediately declared free.

Further, the British government had, one year before introducing the Abolition Act, made provision to compensate slave owners for the impending loss of their "property". The bill for this came to £20 million

– £16 billion today, adjusted for inflation – and it is one that the British taxpayer was lumbered with paying for until 2015. Nothing was ever offered to the slaves themselves to make up for their suffering.

Impacts of the Slavery Abolition Act

Even after the Act's introduction in 1984, it was not so simple as former slaves now being able to live freely overnight. First, there was the apprenticeship system, which was a way for planters to keep former slaves on at a much lower rate than proper employment would afford them. It was a system doomed to failure, for the planters resented having to pay even a modest amount for services they once enjoyed for free. Either they felt it was not an economically viable proposition, or some refused to use it out of a point of principle. And, even when offered, it was hardly an enticing deal for the workers, either. It was low-paid work in scarcely better conditions than they had been experienced as slaves, and there was no guarantee of contracted employment at the end of it. Not to mention, once offered the opportunity of even a paid role, many former slaves were loath to return to the industry and employers under whom they had previously endured such brutalities.

The planter class defended, through economic charts, the need to retain slavery. They pointed out that paying wages to ex-slaves or appointing paid labourers to do the same job they were accustomed to having done for free would gravely affect the economy. Other issues the planters had to face were estate mismanagement in the face of owner absenteeism.

Moreover, planters had borrowed much from British merchants and many now found themselves unable to repay their debts due to low returns. In a vicious circle, many continued to borrow from them in an attempt to resurrect their plantations, only deepening their debts further. West Indian banks and commercial companies, on the other hand, were hesitant to lend to planters. The British Guiana Bank and the Planters' Bank of Jamaica, for example, were no longer interested in estates as collateral for loans, and the Colonial Bank of the West Indies refused to offer large loans to planters.

At the same time as objections were being raised to paying former slaves, many of these former slaves were themselves migrating in vast numbers away from farms in the more populous colonies, leading to a shortage of consistent, relatively inexpensive labour even for those who were willing to employ it.

The British ban had knock-on effects across the Caribbean, with similar acts being passed in the Caribbean territories of Denmark and France (where Napoleon had reintroduced slavery in 1802) in 1848 and the Netherlands in 1863, and also made things more difficult for North American planters.

Slavery was already firmly established in colonial North America by the eighteenth century and continued after the United States' founding in 1776, peaking in the nineteenth century and then enduring a precipitous decline until its abolition in 1865, more than 30 years after Britain.

By the 1800s, the slave population in the United States had exploded. In the early eighteenth century, they numbered fewer than 10,000; a hundred years later, a total of more than 300,000 Africans had been captured and taken to the US, and as these slaves typically spent the remainder of their lives there, and had families, meaning generation after generation were born into slavery, the slave population grew to 800,000 by 1800.

When the time came for the American trade to be banned, it proved even more difficult than it had for the British. The sheer size of the slave population was part of the reason for this, as well as the much greater landmass they were distributed across, compared to the small islands of the Caribbean colonies. That America's slave trade happened largely within its own boundaries also made abolishment of, and reparation for, slavery that much more complicated. The legacy of slavery inside the United States, and the grievances of both sides making bitter enemies of two races who had to continue living together as countrymen, can at least partly account for ethnic and class divisions which persist in the US to this day, affecting millions of individuals.

British involvement at the time in what is now the continental United States added to the complications of banning slavery in America and may partly explain why it took the US so much longer to outlaw the practice. While British-Caribbean slaveholders were compensated in the wake of abolition, their counterparts in British North America were not. The Act did, however, establish Canada – then a British colony – as a free territory for American-based slaves, whether those emancipated in 1834 from British North America or refugees from farms in the United States. Starting in 1834 and for the next quarter-century or so, thousands of escaped and freed African slaves crossed the border into Canada.

Canada's own anti-slavery sentiment had been gathering pace in tandem with Britain's, especially in Upper Canada, a division of British Canada which roughly covered what is now Ontario. Within two years, in its second legislative session, Upper Canada passed the Act to Limit Slavery in the region. While this did not free any existing slaves, it outlawed any further importation of them, and granted freedom to any children of slaves automatically upon reaching the age of 25.

Abolitionist efforts in the eastern provinces of Lower Canada (now Québec), Nova Scotia and New Brunswick, on the other hand, failed. Lower Canada politician Pierre-Louis Panet, for example, proposed in the National Assembly in 1793 – the same year that Upper Canada passed its Act to Limit Slavery – to abolish enslavement in his province, but despite the issue lingering for several sessions, it was never voted on. However, Upper Canada remained an attractive destination for refugee slaves in 1834, given its promised freedoms and its land border with the United States.

The British Empire had a unique functional identity thanks to the mercantilist era's independent and competitive imperialisms, and had advanced through successive stages of commercial and industrial capitalism ahead of others. However, separating the transition of a slave labour system in the British colonies from later processes elsewhere is artificial, and this is made all the more unacceptable by the general decline of mercantilism, the progressive spread of free trade and laissez-faire principles, and the concurrent substitution of an intensifying capitalist system across much of the world.

But a large part of the economy of Britain and other nations still depended on the crops that the slaves had tended. Consequently, even with slavery abolished and slave masters financially assuaged, this was not the end of the saga of human cargo. Planters still had to find a way to continue output and generate profit so that their livelihoods, at least so far as they were accustomed to, could be maintained.

With free labour no longer at their disposal, a new system was petitioned for – and the British government gladly helped them establish one. This was what led to indenture – a new form of exploitation which carried a different name and which trained its sights on a different part of the world for recruitment, but which largely resembled the practices which had preceded it. This was indentured labour, introduced in 1835, with the first Indians arriving in the Caribbean under this new system later that year.

INDENTURE: SLAVERY BY ANOTHER NAME

"With few exceptions, they are handled with unreasonable severity, with overwork and personal chastisement."

While you might expect this quote to be referring to the experience of slaves, of Africans, during the ghastly peak of the trade, it was not. These words were uttered, by British special magistrate Charles Anderson, in reference to contemporary events in 1838, a full five years after slavery was ostensibly abolished. He was telling Lord Stanley, Secretary of State for the Colonies, about what was happening to those poor souls who had been duped into signing up for backbreaking labour and human rights abuses half a world away – the indentured workers of South Asia, who had replaced the African slaves, but who were treated much the same.

If there could be any doubt as to the harshness of the conditions these workers endured, and the disdain with which their lives were treated, consider another quote, this time from historian Hugh Tinker, writing in 1974 in his book, *A New System of Slavery: The Export of Indian Labor Overseas, 1830-1970*:

"The rotting bones of immigrants were regularly unearthed in cane fields."

This brief but brutal sentence could not have better summed up the true nature of indenture if it had run to many more words.

Indentured labour was approved by Britain in 1833, the same year the Slavery Abolition Act was drawn up, with the government fully aware they would need something similar in place if sugar and other crops in the Caribbean and other colonial regions were to remain profitable. Sugar production continued to serve as the economic backbone of the British Empire, and the imperial political economy relied heavily on labour-intensive agriculture. But indenture did not quite provide the hoped-for solution, coming as it did at a time of great uncertainty for the Empire.

The emancipation of slaves was met with great resistance from the planter class, and the apprenticeship system that was supposed to ease the transition from slavery to free labour had been an abject failure, leading to its cancellation in 1839.

Economic conditions in the Caribbean colonies were deteriorating steadily, worsened by the fast growth of new sugar plantation areas in Cuba and Brazil, which continued to employ slaves, as well as Mauritius and eastern India, and by the rising popularity of beet sugar, which was cheaper to produce and came from a more geographically versatile plant than cane sugar.

This already fraught situation was worsened considerably when the British government introduced the Sugar Duties Act in 1946, which equalised taxes on sugar imported from the colonies. Previously, Caribbean planters had enjoyed reduced import duties and had been led to believe this would remain in place as a compromise for them agreeing to the abolishment of slavery. Guarantees that had been in place of a certain amount of colonial sugar being purchased by Britain were also lifted. The British government was seeking to capitalise on the surging demand for sugar across Europe, realising that it couldn't possibly hope for a piece of this action without going the free trade route, since buyers inevitably sought out the lowest prices, and these could not be offered under Britain's existing system.

With no tax breaks, the near-impossibility of competing with many rival nations and territories, and beet sugar being grown in Europe, the Caribbean planters, especially in the older colonies of Jamaica, Antigua, St Vincent and Grenada, appeared doomed. But they weren't going to give up without a fight. Mass protests against free trade broke out in the West Indies, led by the plantocracy, who at the same time immersed themselves in efforts to restructure their production technologies and techniques to keep their crops financially viable and enable them to compete in the open global market. Among these strategies was to extract as much "return on investment" as humanly possible from their indentured employees, wringing every last drop of effort from them for as little expenditure as they could get away with, and working them – sometimes literally – into the ground.

The beginnings of indenture

The first territory to receive a consignment of South Asian indentured workers was not in the Caribbean bur rather the Indian Ocean, namely Mauritius, which since 1810 had been a colony of Britain – its last of three overseas rulers, following the Netherlands (1598-1710) and France (1715-1810), having been discovered in 1507 by the Portuguese, who were otherwise not interested in such small and isolated islands, especially since it had already established bigger and more populous territories on the African mainland.

Slavery was a well established, albeit divisive, practice in Mauritius, which was also seeing a boom in sugar exports. At its peak, slaves numbered some 80 per cent (or 60,000) of the islands' population in the late 1700s, though the trade was the subject of political infighting when the French government attempted to ban slavery there, triggering a secessionist movement in 1796.

When Britain assumed control of Mauritius following victory in a raid conducted during the Napoleonic Wars, the islands' new rulers found a steep pyramidical society in place. At the thin top of this power structure was a tiny elite of white French landowners, merchants, officials and professionals. Although the British had secured Mauritius by force, to effectively manage the islands they required the cooperation of the Franco-Mauritian landowners, who provided them with security and markets in exchange for commodities which were scarce in the small, isolated territory. These wealthy elites presided over a small middle-class demographic comprised of craftsmen of mixed ancestry, while at the bottom, and by far the most numerous, was a large population of black slaves, most of whom had been brought in from Madagascar, Mozambique and Zanzibar. But once slavery was abolished by its new rulers – Mauritius being the last of the British colonies to do so, on February 1, 1835 – it would be the South Asian indentured labourers that replaced them who would find themselves at the bottom of the islands' pecking order.

Even before slavery was stopped, Mauritius had been enduring a severe labour shortage in the sugar sector. It had become the colony's economic mainstay and was rapidly expanding as demand for the crop grew, but its relatively small population struggled to keep up, even if the large majority of this population were slaves, since mortality rates among slaves were far exceeding births. The introduction of indentured workers, then, was most welcome, and began in earnest, with the first of them arriving in Port Louis, six weeks after departing from Calcutta, on November 2, 1834. From this point on, until 1917 when indenture was abolished, more than 450,000 Indians set sail for Mauritius, where they imagined – and were told – they would find financial comfort.

The Indian workers did indeed help Mauritius – and therefore the British Empire – maintain a foothold in the international sugar race, and beyond that the Indians have played an enormous part in shaping the islands' development and culture. While indenture is a tragic period in Indian history, for Mauritius November 2, 1834, was a momentous occasion, and its legacy is celebrated with a national holiday on that date every year.

A new form of slavery spreads

At the time indenture was being rolled out in Mauritius, Sir John Gladstone, the father of future Prime Minister William Gladstone, owned sugar plantations in Jamaica and British Guiana. In the latter, the Demerara Rebellion broke out on his Demerara-Essequibo plantation in 1823. Though it was quickly put down by the British Army, it was one of several key revolts during a time of growing discontentment with slavery, so Gladstone knew as well as anybody the importance of preparing for a post-slavery future – even if he was to benefit enormously from the programme of compensation offered to planters, so large was the number of slaves he owned. Reparation for the loss of the services of more than 2,500 slaves netted Gladstone a total of £106,769 – more than £10 million in 2023, adjusted for inflation. This was the biggest such payout of them all.

Gladstone had watched with great interest the developments in Mauritius and was much enthused by what he saw unfolding there. He decided this was the answer in the Caribbean, too, and set about seducing a new workforce. He wrote in January 1836 to the agency of Gillanders, Arbuthnot & Co in Calcutta, the same firm which was handling the Mauritius programme, to enquire about the feasibility of replicating the model in another part of the world – the Caribbean. In doing so, Gladstone rather fancifully promised any such workers sent to his plantations could expect education, health care, fair pay and light work. None of this was true, and those unfortunate enough to respond to Gladstone's overtures were to find their experience little different to that of the slaves they were replacing.

The agency, oblivious to the realities of Gladstone's businesses – and in any case cooperative as they, too, were making money by capitalising on this new trade – were agreeable, writing back: "We are not aware that any greater difficulty would present itself in sending men to the West Indies, the natives being perfectly ignorant of the place they go to or the length of the voyage they are undertaking."

The recruitment of South Asian indentured labourers to the Caribbean enthusiastically began. The exact date and port of disembarkation of the first batch varies depending on the source, but it is generally accepted as having happened later that same year, 1836.

A civil contract between Britain and Indian labourers was written up for an initial duration of five years under a programme established by Lord Stanley, Secretary of State for the Colonies. The labourers would be confined to their assigned farms and given a meagre daily wage of one shilling (£11.50 in 2024). Any violation of contract would result in an automatic penalty of two months in jail or a fine of £5 (£475 in 2024). It would not be wrong to say that Indians were treated much as enslaved Africans had been: inhumanely and cold-bloodedly. The pittance they were paid, and the fact they had initially consented to their presence, did not change this.

It wasn't long, however, before this was noticed. In 1838, a special magistrate, Charles Anderson, wrote to Lord Stanley, stating in refence to the indentured workers that "with few exceptions, they are handled with unreasonable severity, with overwork and personal chastisement".

If labourers did not work, they were not paid or fed, and they would die of starvation. According to historian Hugh Tinker, writing in *A New System of Slavery: The Export of Indian Labor Overseas 1830-1920*, in 1974: "The rotting bones of immigrants were regularly unearthed in cane fields."

Other colonial powers across the Caribbean and elsewhere – most notably South Africa, Fiji and Reunion – similarly adjusting to a post-slavery world, also began implementing indentureship and recruiting from India, though they too were doing so in an inhumane manner. What was being presented as a palatable alternative to slavery was anything but, though at least now greater scrutiny was being applied to plantation management and abuses were no longer tolerated the way they once were. Several Caribbean territories were denied further shipments of labour as reports surfaced of the ill-treatments there. For instance, the Danish plantation in St Croix – then part of the Danish West Indies, and now in the US Virgin Islands – was reportedly so brutal to its workers that the Indian government cancelled its contract of labourer shipment after a single voyage.

Still, the system continued until 1917, when Britain's Imperial Legislative Council banned indenture. It is widely thought, though, that this ban was enacted not out of concerns over human rights, but because indenture was declining in profitability.

Why were South Asians targeted?

Mauritius had led by example in its import of indentured labourers, showing how Indians and other South Asians were a perfect fit for the scheme, and leading to them then being sent to the Caribbean and elsewhere. But why was this so? Why did they appeal to planters, and more to the point, why did indentured work appeal to South Asians? After all, this was not – at least at the recruitment stage – like slavery, in that they had to go of their own accord. This question is asked not just with the benefit of hindsight and knowing how they suffered, but even if we were to accept that they signed up for the programme in the belief they would be treated and recompensed fairly, it is still a huge undertaking and commitment to leave your homeland, family and friends, even for work, especially as it was largely a journey into the unknown. The voyage from India to the Caribbean generally took three to four months on ships carrying more than 500 migrants. The average sex ratio was three males to one female, and most of them were in their 20s. As a result of unhygienic conditions, malnutrition and poor management, cholera was rife.

First of all, we have to bear in mind that the conditions at home were often poor for many South Asians. As is typically the case even today, people do not tend to migrate unless they believe better conditions await them elsewhere. In the nineteenth century, parts of India were being racked by consecutive famines, a lot of local industries were relocating to urban centres, and unemployment was snowballing. To the poor, hungry or unemployed, the prospect of a steady income for a set period of time

48

might have sounded very appealing, even if it meant moving across oceans to pursue it.

It is also fair to say a certain amount of duplicity was at play in the recruitment process, too. Many of the individuals courted for indentureship were ill-educated or even illiterate, with little knowledge of the wider world and thus where they were being sent and, in some cases, unable to read the documents they were signing. This meant the recruiters could remain free of accusations the whole thing was a scam, because they did after all have a paper trail they could point to in their defence – but in targeting those who didn't really know what this paper trail meant, they were guilty at the very least of a level of cynical manipulation. That's how a gigantic number of Indian men, women and children were trapped into indenture and exploited ruthlessly to produce rum, sugar and other popular industrial products of that time.

The major portion of expenditures of recruitment and migration from India to the Caribbean was handled by colonial governments, and planters had to pay a significant share of these costs. Emigrant agencies sought recruits from all across the Indian countryside under licence from the procurers of migrants in Madras and Calcutta.

These emigrant agencies recruited the labour systematically and geographically. In the early years, they selected men, women and children from tribal areas and urban peripheries. In later decades, rural hinterlands were the main recruiting sites.

Imagine a sponge being squeezed until the last drop of water is wrung out of it – that's how the British planter class extracted people from India to serve them at wages that were insufficient and unjust.

THE LEGACY OF INDENTURE: INDIAN INFLUENCE IN THE MODERN CARIBBEAN

For those who endured it, indenture was a terrible business. The human rights abuses of the system are undeniable. And yet, positives arose from the practice – not that this will be of any consolation to those who suffered, or their ancestors who continue to struggle even today as "others" in the land of their birth, where their grandparents or great-grandparents had alighted without really knowing what they and their future generations had been tricked into.

The positives, though, were first of all economic. Of course, the planters who employed indentured labourers benefitted personally – not that this is something which should be celebrated. But the wider economies of the territories and nations enjoyed an uptick in sugar production – and consequently incomes – once indenture had been introduced. Productivity shot up, even without more land being put to use. By 1860, output of sugar and other exported staples exceeded even the levels achieved during slavery. This rebound can be directly ascribed to the contribution of Indian labour, which had knock-on effects of spurring development and improving infrastructure, even as the pressures of free trade and rising competition were being felt. And then, as most indentured workers settled in the lands they had been taken to – either by choice or necessity, when they found a return to India might be problematic – and raised further generations there, these countries and territories grew to become richly multicultural, with these significant South Asian immigrant populations living alongside indigenous people, colonial and ex-colonial Europeans, emancipated Africans, and Chinese who had either relocated deliberately as merchants or who had similarly been brought in under other indentureship programmes.

Such mixing of people can create various industries and revenue streams as different cultures, business practices and consumer behaviours all bring their own influences to bear, but on the other hand, racial tensions too are often inevitable in multicultural societies, with an "us and them" mentality separating natives and incomers, and rivalries between different immigrant groups, and some migrants – or descendants of migrants – struggling to establish their own identities, finding they are considered outsiders both where they live and where they (or their forebears) are from.

Regardless, the territories which had brought in South Asian indentured labourers – most notably the Caribbean, as well as Mauritius, Fiji and South Africa – couldn't fail to be grateful for how these immigrants had helped turned their economic fortunes around, and for the contribution they have made, and continue to make, to their societies, and several of them give thanks for this with national holidays. For example, Guyana observes Indian Arrival Day every May 5, which was the day in 1838 when the SS Hesperus and SS Whitby ships arrived in Berbice and Demerara, respectively, with a combined 396 Indians on board. In Mauritius, where the population today is almost 66 per cent Indian ethnicity, the Anniversary of the Arrival of Indentured Labourers is marked on November 2, the day in 1834 when L'Atlas docked in Port Louis with 36 workers from Calcutta – Britain's first consignment of indentured labourers. Similar holidays are observed in Trinidad and Tobago (May 30), Jamaica (May 10), Grenada (May 1), St Lucia (May 6), St Vincent and the Grenadines (Indian Arrival Day on June 1 and Indian Heritage Day on October 7), Suriname (June 5), Fiji (May 14) and South Africa (November 16).

Indians had already left an unmistakeable mark on the Caribbean over the nearly nine-decade-long indenture period, not only due to their efforts in stabilising the sugar industry, but also in terms of their social and cultural contribution, and this would increase after Britain abolished Indian indenture in 1917 (though the practice continued until the early 1920s). Once freed from the bonds of indenture, those Indians who had made the Caribbean their home and had elected to stay could now pursue other commercial avenues, as well as branch out geographically. Some continued to work as regular employees on the plantations, but many took work in other industries or set up their own businesses. As they did so, and as they put down roots in these strange lands, their cultural influence began to spread. Temples and mosques were built, while the music, dress and other customs of South Asia became more regular sights, their native languages were heard in wider society, and their food grew popular with locals and other immigrants, either in its own right or as an influence on indigenous cuisines.

During indenture, the Indians had worked tirelessly to secure the sugar sector's survival and also played a major role in the rapid rise of rice farming. They contributed heavily to rural development and the cultivation of cash crops. Once their contracts ended, those who elected not to renew but to stay put often moved, from the late 1880s onward, into other manual fields, such as boat-building, charcoal-making, fishing, animal husbandry or small-scale manufacturing, or into the service sector, for example as cab drivers and porters. They understood the importance of education for their children, and with the immigrants' presence boosting labour supply, there were more opportunities to pursue it. Their descendants often took on academic and vocational training, the next generation becoming teachers, bankers, carpenters, tailors, merchants, physicians, solicitors, accountants and clerical workers, among others.

Today, modern Indo-Caribbeans continue to make great contributions to economic, social and cultural development, and the pursuit and delivery of education, and are proving influential in politics, business, medicine, sports, media and, unsurprisingly, labour unions. They are a big part of everyday life.

This is an extension of the reasons why Indians were favoured for indenture in the first place, and why their involvement in it proved a success for the planters. Their cultural qualities of tenacity and perseverance, their respect for customs and tradition, and their dedication to family where among the traits that fostered thrift, industry and self-esteem, which helped them succeed as indentured workers, and which help them succeed today. It is, in some ways, similar to how modern-day African-Americans are often sound physical specimens, making up a greater percentage of US athletes than other ethnicities. Many are the descendants of North American and Caribbean slaves, who only survived if they were fit and strong. With the South Asian indentured labourers, those who survived and thrived were usually the more ingenious of their number.

It is, though, important not to stereotype. While the positive outcomes of this "survival of the fittest" trend can be identified, the planters were guilty of pigeonholing migrants along more critical lines. Discourses from the time sought to characterise Indian "coolies" and African "negroes", the former mocked as docile and obedient even if their diligence and cleverness was recognised, while the blacks were drawn up as luxury-loving, indolent and immoral.

Unfortunately, as can happen with stereotypes, they can be assumed by some to be accurate and natural descriptions of certain ethnic groups, while the unique colonial past that led to the formation of such rhetoric is forgotten or ignored.

Exploitation of the caste system

A major reason why there was little outcry over South Asian indenture at the time, and why in the present day the history of indenture is not as reviled as that of slavery, is, simply put, due to ignorance. There was ignorance at the time over the true nature of the system, and over the reasons why Indians took part in it. There was a certain level of ignorance behind why so few of the Indians who signed up for indenture later returned home. And there is a near-total ignorance today even among Indians themselves about the history of indenture and why there is such a large Indian diaspora in certain countries. On that note, many Indians are ignorant about the sheer numbers of their kinfolk abroad, and of the differences between these two demographics who are essentially the same people but who have been culturally separated for decades or centuries. But this is an ignorance which cannot, for the most part, be blamed on the shortcomings of individuals or groups. Rather, it stems from the fact that, in the current day, the history of indenture is something that is scarcely taught in India (or elsewhere, for that matter), and that during the active period of indenture itself, the ignorance of Indians was something very deliberately cultivated by the colonial powers.

This was part of a "divide and rule" strategy similar to that which had been enacted inside India by the British, now being played out in the Caribbean territories.

Bear in mind that the indenture programme was brought in during a time of rising Indian dissatisfaction with British rule (which also followed the opposition to slavery that eventually led to that industry's abolition). Indentureship proved an important tool in British efforts to quell rebellion sentiment, as it could break up communities, transport people thousands of miles, make correspondence with their homeland and relatives there extremely difficult if not downright impossible, erect barriers to any return, and fray or even completely sever ties with the Indian homeland by employing misinformation designed to erode sympathy and sentiment between Indians separated by oceans.

The exploitation of Indian labour could continue beyond the mere cynical method of their recruitment, for once these workers had arrived in these foreign lands, it was easy to keep them there. Yes, they had signed contracts with an end date, but the indentured Indians often experienced the revocation of these contracts, leaving them without legal recourse, or the changing of rules and regulations, aimed at frustrating any attempt to go home. This way, not only did Britain ensure it always had a labour supply, but it also kept a people subjugated and divided, thus reducing any threat of a unified approach to rebellion. Most indentured workers were even prohibited from sending or receiving letters to and from India, causing many families to lose contact and leaving many migrants feeling they could no longer return home, even if they were able to – a situation worsened by widespread relocations inside India as people were either forced by the British to move, or chose to do so to evade punishment if suspected of acting against British rule or interests. Furthermore, great efforts were made in the colonies to repress Indian languages, culture, religions and customs, so that subsequent generations of Indo-Caribbeans were distanced further still from their forebears.

Indentureship also proved a handy way to deal with convicts, and most particularly any who had been involved in mutinous activities. What better way to deal with elements disruptive to British rule than by removing them completely; transplanting them thousands of miles so that there would be no chance of them influencing anyone at home?

What had started as a means of procuring cheap labour was now also being used as a strategy to suppress Indian rebellion, particularly in the wake of the 1857 outbreak of the Sepoy Mutiny, named after the Persian-derived word for soldier, which was widely used in India at the time. These soldiers, though officially part of the British army, led a rebellion which, while unsuccessful, took more than two years to put down. Those who were convicted of playing any part in mutinous activities were typically sent to work overseas. Administrative records from the time in both Britain and India show that from 1857 onwards, incarcerated convicts were the preferred source of indentured labour sent to the Caribbean, the Andaman Islands, Mauritius and Fiji. There were clear parallels here with the well-documented transportation of British convicts to Australia, which had begun in the late eighteenth century and was ongoing at this time.

As the British considered who else might prove seditious, *brahmins* and *khsatriyas* were particularly targeted because, as Hindu priests and warriors, respectively, they represented an influential counterweight to the British authority's application of Christian missionary activities to undermine India's traditional cultures and faiths. Consequently, many Indians changed their names and castes in an attempt to avoid punishment at the hands of the British.

Caste, however, was something that the British exploited too, as they understood its role in rigid social hierarchies in India, and how this could be taken advantage of as part of efforts to divide a people that was growing increasingly unified in anti-colonial sentiment.

The Hindu caste system, which dates back more than 3,000 years, was originally comprised of just four castes – *brahmins*, *kshatriyas*, *vaishyas* (merchants) and *shudras* (artisans and labourers) – but in modern India there are thousands. Many of these, however, were created by the British as a means to not only formerly identify all Indians in official records but to also assign them a place in society from which they would tend not to stray – which, in theory, would discourage them from joining the revolution. For example, whereas it had previously sufficed to have one overall merchant caste (the *vaishyas*), this was now splintered into a vast number of specific other castes, depending on what they sold – oil, cloth, jewellery, vegetables and so on.

However, since the British hadn't enacted this new caste system *before* they started sending Indians overseas, it was not something that really transferred in practice to the Caribbean. As a result, Indo-Caribbeans have since developed a culture of their own which is quite different to that of Indians in India itself, and one that is often not as tightly bound to social differences.

Differences between Indians and Indo-Caribbeans

While the history of indenture remains largely untaught in the official curricula of India and elsewhere, among those who do study and disseminate it, Professor Kapil Kumar is arguably the foremost authority on the Indo-Caribbean experience, both historically and how it is lived today, and what he calls the "suppressed realities" of Indian history.

Prof Kumar has lived in, travelled around and written about many of the destinations to where indentured Indians were sent, as well as teaching and speaking in these same places and elsewhere. He has extensively interviewed Indians both in their homeland and overseas and organised visits in either direction to encourage greater awareness of indenture and to repair or re-establish ties.

His efforts in the latter regard were inspired by how, as he studied the differences between native and diasporic Indians, he became increasingly aware of the striking lack of knowledge homeland Indians had about their Caribbean counterparts. He has examined carefully this phenomenon of how most Indians know very little, if anything, about Indo-Caribbean people, and how some are even astonished to learn that Indians reside in significant numbers in that part of the world. Even those who are aware of this typically imagine Indo-Caribbeans are new or first-generation migrants, and their cultural frame of reference can sometimes not extend much beyond the handful of ethnic Indians they have seen playing cricket for the West Indies.

This, Prof Kumar believes, is a legacy of the British "divide and rule" strategy, which most obviously manifests in the near-total absence from Indian classrooms of any teaching of indentureship history, but also in the many deliberate falsehoods propagated by the British that are taken to be true even by those few who are aware of it – usually the descendants of Indians who had been taken away to work.

Among the myths about indentureship, Indian indentured workers and the Indian culture of the time are those such as: Most Indians then were low caste; India was poor and so its people were happy to leave;

early Indian migrants did not want to return; once an Indian Hindu crossed the sea, their caste was broken and they could not return; only poor people left India; people left because of casteism, fatalism and Hindu beliefs; and it was good that they left, because only backward people stayed in India. But despite these beliefs having been taught even by prominent academics, they were all wrong.

For a start, we must take issue with the prevailing image of India in the nineteenth century as a poor and backward place. Logically, this could not have been true, because if it was, why would Britain have coveted this territory and invested so heavily in it, even going so far as to call the subcontinent its "Crown Jewel" or "The Jewel of the British Empire"? Such phrases could only be applied to a prosperous land, especially at a time when the Empire stretched far and wide and touched every corner of the globe. And it can certainly be argued that subsequent poverty in certain regions of India, which admittedly is evident today, is a result of the "scorched earth" policy employed by Britain in retaliation to those who fought for independence, particularly in the north, and the widespread looting by the British of India's natural resources. (Something that Prof Kumar found Indo-Caribbeans were largely unaware of, demonstrating how this cultivated ignorance of a shared history applied in both directions).

This two-way ignorance of each other's realities is a direct result of Britain's successful efforts to divide Indians. The aforementioned obstacles to migrants returning home or even maintaining contact with their relatives meant many indentured workers settled in these foreign lands and built new families of their own.

Now, generations later, they are in many ways a distinct people, while their kinfolk in India may be completely unaware of this branch of their bloodline.

There are now some significant differences between Indians and their Indo-Caribbean counterparts as a result of this nineteenth-century upheaval and its subsequent ramifications. For a start, native languages such as Hindi, Urdu, Awadhi, Brij, Basha, Bhojpuri and more are relatively rarely spoken in the West Indies. Homeland Indians may frown on this, without considering it is a result of colonial suppression of mother tongues.

On the other hand, while traditional languages have been threatened or lost, some aspects of "old style" India remain in the Caribbean. For example, the Hinduism practised there is seen as highly traditional, as it retains many of the traditions that date back some 180 years or more to the start of indenture, when the labourers took their faith with them to smaller, more isolated lands where it was less susceptible to the influences of a far larger country and population such as the homeland. Furthermore, the original castes have largely been retained – again, because they were what the migrants took with them, and because the British multiplication of castes did not take hold in the islands.

One thing that the Indo-Caribbeans have largely cast aside, though, is a society based along class, wealth or colour lines. If their relocation was a "reset" of sorts, it allowed for exposure to other peoples and for a greater freedom of spirit. For example, many Indo-Caribbeans see the practice of arranged marriages as anachronistic and appreciate being able to choose partners for reasons apart from caste and social status. Furthermore, daughters carry the same status as sons, and so dowries tend not to be a consideration in any marriage. Indo-Caribbeans also consider discussions of income and displays of wealth to be in bad taste, and they do not attach stigma to darker skin colours.

Accordingly, many Indians consider their Caribbean counterparts to be "too western", or even see them as poor and unattractive, and would like to see them more widely adopt traditional Indian ways. And yet, Indo-Caribbeans often find the governments and indigenous people of their adopted homelands not western *enough*. Even in highly multicultural countries such as Jamaica, Trinidad, Guyana and Suriname, South Asians – even those families which have been there for nearly two centuries, or even those of mixed Indian and black race – are still regarded simply as "Indian" rather than Indo-Caribbean or creole. Sadly, many have distanced themselves further from their roots. In an attempt to fit in, they have eschewed languages, changed religions and otherwise behaved in a way designed to ingratiate themselves with their "hosts".

This is the contemporary legacy of indenture: millions of people left feeling culturally homeless; too foreign for the land in which they were born, and too foreign for the land from which their ancestors came. This explains why many Indo-Caribbeans have felt compelled to migrate again, often to North America or Europe, to where they imagine they can escape from such prejudice. Of course, many find that is also a false hope, and it has put yet another generation and thousands more miles between them and their forebears.

DOCUMENTING REALITY: EXISTING MATERIAL

It is said that history is written by the victors. Who actually said it first is not known, but it was a line famously recited by Winston Churchill, and before him, Hermann Göring. Regardless of its origins, it is a popular quote because of its accuracy. One of the rewards for victory –whatever the means used in its pursuit – is the "right" to tell the story of how that victory was achieved. Or, when it is convenient to do so, to suppress the story of the struggle altogether.

That is perhaps why the tale of Indian indenture is so little known. While Britain has long since ceased the practice, the fact it was allowed to continue for so long, that it has never been held up as an atrocity in the same way slavery has been, that nobody has ever been held to account for the suffering inflicted on humans under this programme, that Britain and its territories benefited economically for this, and that those who were deceived and abused were never compensated, can certainly be considered a victory of sorts. Consequently, what little has been written about indenture has, for the most part and until relatively recently, been written by the victors. Inevitably, this has constructed a largely positive narrative of indenture, at the same time as deliberate and successful efforts were made to keep indentured labourers separated from their Indian homeland – both physically and socially – to ensure little was known of their fate by those they left behind. This has resulted in a lack of communal memory and explains why there has been little outrage and a lack of desire to know more.

Of course, indenture was a big, state-run business, and so records exist, as do other official documents, but there was relatively little commentary published at the time or in the years that followed, and what was written tended to be by those directly involved (in other words, those who benefitted from indenture), or by colonial supporters. Even those who have sought to write the histories of the subjugated have been largely limited to the colonisers' documents for their source material, which inevitably leads to a biased telling. Others missed the crucial window available to them to secure the oral histories of indenture survivors, meaning they were left with the anecdotal material of their successors.

Those seeking to learn more about Indian indenture will find that two publications have dominated the modern field. While both have their flaws, *A New System of Slavery* by Hugh Tinker (1974), and *A Question of Labour* (1994) by KO Laurence, remain by far the most comprehensive studies to date on this subject.

Laurence's book looks at the migration and settlement of Indians in the Caribbean. He demonstrates how indenture was arranged via a three-way interaction between the British and Indian governments, the administrations of the British Caribbean territories, and plantation owners. His study, stretching to nearly 650 pages, is information-dense and was compiled over a period of almost 30 years, but is regrettably lacking in quoted testimony. Given that Laurence began his research in the 1960s, when there were still surviving indentured labourers living in British Guiana (as Guyana was still called until gaining independence in 1970) and Trinidad and Tobago, his work would have offered an even more complete picture had it included their oral histories.

At least *A Question of Labour* offers a contradictory perspective to the pro-colonial texts and, when it was finally delivered after decades of promise, it was welcomed in both Caribbean and Indian academia. More critical still was *A New System of Slavery*, published 20 years earlier, and yet even in 1974 – well over half a century on from the end of indenture – this was the first major historical study of its kind. In this, Tinker looks at the supply of Indian labour to the Caribbean, Mauritius, South and East Africa and elsewhere in the post-slavery environment, and comes to the conclusion that it was a system which barely differed from its predecessor.

Tinker paints a grim picture of the conditions endured by Indian labourers and says they were identical to those experienced by African slaves, and it is his contention that indentureship simply replaced one oppressive practice with another, with indentured workers mistreated for decades on sugar plantations. However, one counterpoint to the critical narrative, which is raised by Tinker himself, is that unlike the African slaves, tens of thousands of indentured Indians elected to continue with this work, renewing their contracts two, three or even four times, even when they were not obliged to, and furthermore many chose to remain in the territories rather than return to India once they were free to do so, some even putting down roots by buying land and setting up businesses. Apologists for indenture may cite this trend as proof that things could not have been so bad after all, though a more careful consideration of the reasons why these Indians chose to stay – as detailed in the previous chapter – would, rather than undermine Tinker's criticisms, actually reinforce them. It is regrettable that Tinker did not explore this more fully. If he had done, he might also have determined that, while certainly there were colonial "divide and conquer" efforts at play, there was also an element of resilience and adaptability in the Indian nature; that the indentured workers, once aware of the true nature of the circumstances they had found themselves in, attempted to make the best of it. Yes, theoretically they had the option – one that was easier said than done – of going home once their contracts had concluded, but on the other hand there was also a drive to plan a better life – for themselves, by investing in land and business, and for their still-indentured brothers and sisters, and the generations that would follow them, by speaking out against the oppressors and employing a variety of resistance methods.

Inevitably, as pioneers of sorts, both Tinker and Laurence were limited in the materials they could consult, having to rely on the archives of colonialists and the written accounts of Christian missionaries and the occasional European traveller. These were all documents created by individuals, some more than others influenced by their own views, and all containing anecdotal rather than analytical evidence. While both texts remain hugely influential and important, the sad reality is both have made a range of omissions (whether deliberately or not) which, despite the authors' attempts at exposing the injustices of indenture, have accentuated the naivete of the original record-makers.

Other important writers and works

If many Indians in the homeland are unaware of what happened in the Caribbean, Indo-Caribbeans are not. This is inevitable, given they are only a few generations removed from the arrival of indentured Indians, and an awareness that they are not members of the native ethnicity of the islands will stir in many a desire to learn more about who they are and where they came from.

Awareness of indenture among Indo-Caribbeans, as well as interest in the land of their roots, has increased in modern times. This awareness was well on the rise by the time of the publication of *A New System of Slavery*, and Tinker's work fired it further. A year later, in 1975, the Trinidadian branch of the University of the West Indies staged the inaugural symposium on East Indians in the Caribbean, as Indians pushed for a dramatic increase in knowledge of indenture and a greater voice for the workers and their descendants. This as an aim was laudable and, since the 1970s, discussion, debate and discourse on indenture has shifted from Eurocentric to endocentric, which again on the surface is a welcome development. But attempts at revisionism, when motivated by emotion, can sometimes be vulnerable to simplification, omission or imbalance. Consequently, many efforts to tell the story of indenture from a subaltern perspective have, rather than uncovering helpful knowledge, produced a gospel of "us against them".

This is amplified by ethnic, cultural and linguistic divisions in many parts of the Caribbean, both between the inhabitants of any given country, or between the countries themselves. Some Caribbean countries are majority black, others more evenly mixed, while some have English as the lingua franca, and their neighbours have French, Spanish or Dutch. These are divisions imposed by colonial powers, which explains the discrepancy and absence of a comparative approach in the examination of indentureship among different Caribbean countries. Patterns of ethnic rivalry and polarisation, separation tendencies, and hegemonic cultural claims have been replicated and perpetuated in modern Caribbean discourse from the colonial period.

Nonetheless, that the texts generated by this approach contradict the official narrative is something to be welcomed, and it is to the credit of the former colonial nations that these works are recognised, given due prominence, and consulted by many academics – in sad contrast to the attitudes in India. Several archives in these territories also retain the original correspondences between imperial and colonial administrations.

Among other key texts tackling indenture from the subaltern perspective are

"Protest Songs of East Indians in British Guiana", by Ved Prakash Vatuk (1964)
This article, published in the quarterly *Journal of American Folklore*, is based on unfiltered Indian sources. Almost a decade after the final cargo of Indians departed for British Guiana in 1955, the author

performed field studies in British Guiana. More than 900 protest songs were recorded by him from descendants of indentured workers, but sadly, just a few of these songs are available today.

The Still Cry: Personal Accounts of East Indians in Trinidad and Tobago During Indentureship, 1845-1917, by Noor Kumar Mahabir (1985).
Trinidad-born anthropologist Mahabir was one of the first writers to give a voice to survivors of indenture, with 15 first-person accounts. Some of them were still alive at the time of Mahabir's study. That he managed this within the 191 pages of his book begs the question as to why KO Laurence could not have done similarly in his near-650-page offering.

Bechu: Bound Coolie Radical in British Guiana 1894-1901, by Clem Seecharan (1999)
Bechu was the first Indian to testify before the Royal Commission, in 1987. He was called to do so because of his penchant for writing to local newspapers to detail the abuses of those involved in indenture and how the collusion between planters and colonial administrators rendered it nigh-on impossible to obtain justice. Seecharan not only characterised the man behind these letters, but also reproduced the letter themselves (and some critical responses).

"The Brown Atlantic: Re-thinking Post-Slavery", by Devi Hardeen (2012)
Writing with poignant relevance from Liverpool, from where some of the earliest ships involved in South Asian indenture set sail, Hardeen – a lecturer in Cultures, Languages and Area Studies at the city's

university – invokes colour in this dissertation to make the point that transatlantic human rights abuses have not been a solely black issue. She points out that while there has been substantial research on the trade of African slaves, there has been virtually nothing on the same to look at how brown people were affected by a very similar system.

Literature of Girmitiya: History, Culture and Identity, edited by Neha Singh and Sajaudeen Chapparban (2023)
Girmitiya is a word for Indian indentured labourers, with its etymology being that "girmit" came from an Indian pronunciation of the word "agreement", referring to the contracts these workers signed. Consequently, a subculture of *girmitiya* developed during indenture, and this book delves into the community, how it was formed, how it has evolved, and how its people continue to struggle for a sense of identity in the lands their ancestors were shipped to centuries ago.

And some other prominent writers and scholars include

Bridget Brereton – Professor Emerita of History at the University of the West Indies in St Augustine who has written or edited a number of books and articles on the social history of the Caribbean and the history of Trinidad and Tobago. She is a regular columnist for the Trinidadian *Daily Express* newspaper.

Maurits Hassankhan – Suriname-based historian who has written extensively on indenture, migration and the Indian diaspora, based at the Department of History in Paramaribo's Anton de Kom University.

Rosemarijn Hoefte – Dutch historian who was appointed Professor in the History of Suriname at the University of Amsterdam in 2017, as a result of her career-long specialism in Caribbean history. Her key work on indenture is *In Place of Slavery: A Social History of British Indian and Javanese Laborers in Suriname* (1998).

Tota Mangar – Historian, university lecturer and *Guyana Chronicle* journalist who specialises in researching and writing about South Asian, East Asian and African communities in Guyana. His grandparents were indentured Indian labourers.

Prabhu P Mohapatra – Professor at the University of Delhi's Department of History who has had more than two dozen academic articles published on indenture and other subjects in the fields of labour and migration. A lot of his work brings to the fore mostly forgotten writings penned by indentured labourers - an important approach which should not be ignored.

Brinsley Samaroo – Retired Professor of History at the University of the West Indies in St Augustine, who has written extensively on the history of Trinidad and Tobago. Most recently he edited *The Blackest Thing in Slavery Was Not the Black Man* (2022) by Eric Williams, an expansive look at non-slavery forms of exploitation that affected South Asian, East Asian and Pacific people. In 2015 he published a collection of photographs by Garnet Ifill depicting the Trinidadian sugar plantations in the mid twentieth century, *Glimpses of the Sugar Industry : The Art of Garnet Ifill.*

The fact that the above list is a near-comprehensive roundup of the leading credible texts on South Asian indenture shows how under-represented the subject is. Many other such works are limited in their scope, focusing on one country or even one island, and in some cases seem to be more a branch of the author's ambition to forge a reputation as a regional historian rather than their area of expertise. In some other cases, there appears to be a deliberately unorthodox style of assessment implemented, perhaps in an attempt to stand out. Either way, objectivity is sometimes compromised with these approaches, which harms their academic and critical credibility. And in many of the more conventional works, they simply rehash the same historical works of a few major academics.

Regardless, such efforts are still to be encouraged, given the paucity of material on indenture, and especially now that the increased relative enthusiasm for the subject – in the Caribbean, at least – since the 1970s is waning. For example, there was an eleven-year gap between publication of Hardeen's 2012 essay and *Literature of Girmitiya*, the most recent major original texts to be published on the subject.

But, as Prof Mohapatra, in particular, has shown, studies continue to reveal obscure and previously undiscovered writings, despite the colonial enterprise having little interest in preserving the voices of indentured workers and their descendants. If the documented experiences were representative of those of the bulk of Indians who migrated to the Caribbean, then the silences of the past are even more relevant for those who were the minority in the system, especially South Indians recruited from the erstwhile Madras presidency, and Muslims recruited from the North. But the ones who did speak out were the ones who influenced the end of indentureship, along with many political and economic factors. Therefore, it is necessary to discuss Indo-Caribbean historiography from the perspective of indentureship if we are to understand its realities.

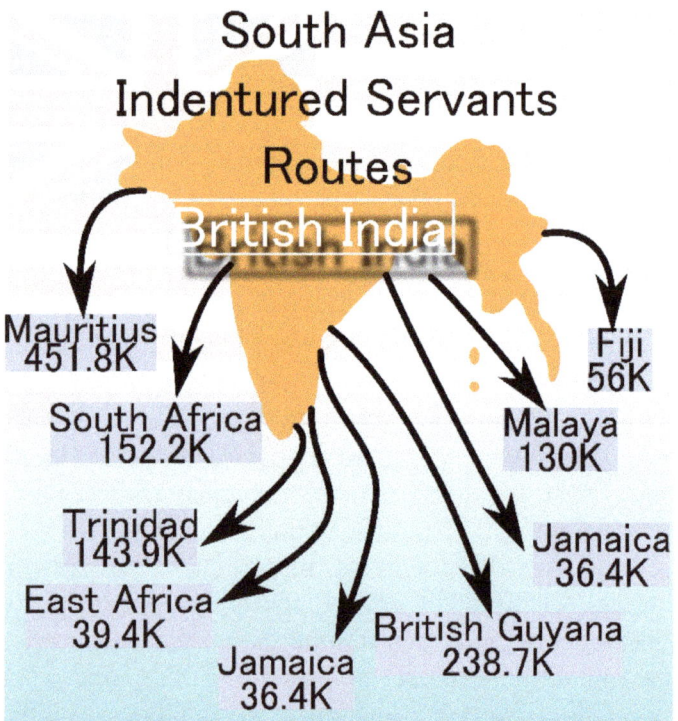

South Asia
Indentured Servants
Routes
British India

Mauritius
451.8K

Fiji
56K

South Africa
152.2K

Malaya
130K

Trinidad
143.9K

Jamaica
36.4K

East Africa
39.4K

British Guyana
238.7K

Jamaica
36.4K

LIFE STORIES:
A CHILD'S ADVENTURE
By curtsey of Oliver Fennell

Don't underestimate the power of a child's imagination.

Often their little minds create whole worlds; places to which they can escape, free from the necessary bounds of childhood, or any difficulties they may be enduring in their real lives. Such worlds have formed the backdrops to some of the classics of children's fiction, whether it was Alice stepping through the Looking Glass, the kids escaping World War II by finding a Lion and a Witch inside a Wardrobe, or a boy discovering Where the Wild Things Are while confined to his bedroom.

Some time around the turn of the twentieth century, in rural India, one little boy also imagined a world in which he could find a better life, an adventure, and an escape. Not much is known about Hunuman Ramoutar's earliest years, other than he lived in poverty in Bihar, and that like most poor people both young and old, he wanted to escape it.

Somewhere, he heard about a world beyond his own; a place where he could make money, where he wouldn't go hungry, where he would have a purpose, and where this would all be in a safe and beautiful setting. To get there, he would have to sail the high seas, but that would only have added to the appeal for a young boy.

And so he set off – on foot, and on his own – to find this fabled new life. He walked the 600km to Kolkata (then Calcutta) in search of one of the ships that would take him there. After this arduous journey – which was only the start – Hunuman found one such ship, and not only that, he was welcomed on to it.

Like the other Indians who would board this ship, Hunuman was required to sign a contract and state his agreement to undertake the voyage and to then work for a set period of time on a sugar plantation upon alighting in Trinidad. He gladly signed this document, despite two factors which highlight the cynicism with which indenture law was practised: one, he was illiterate, and so couldn't possibly understand what he was agreeing to; and two, he was just ten years old.

That a ten-year-old runaway was considered fair game for recruitment into hard labour in a foreign land, unaccompanied by parents or guardians, tells you all you need to know about the mindset of those behind indenture.

Almost a century and half later, Hunuman's eldest grandson, Bharrath, who was born and raised in Trinidad as the first child of Hunuman's first son, remains in awe of not only the initiative young Hunuman showed, but also of the life he set up and legacy he established once his period of indenture was over.

"I do remember him," says Bharrath, "and I can remember his cremation. He died in 1967. I was five years old.

"I didn't hear his story from him, but my father would take me on these little journeys for meetings with older heads, and we'd listen to the stories told by my grandfather's close friends. What I heard from them was that when my grandfather was ten years old, he heard of a ship that takes you to a better life. He walked for a week, from his hometown to the sea, to find the ship.

"They called the journey *kalapani* [black water]. He didn't know it, but it was a very treacherous journey. I understand a lot of people died, because it was a lot longer than the trip from [West] Africa to the Caribbean, going around the Cape of Good Hope. He was on his own; I think he was very brave."

That is beyond dispute, and this fighting spirit already evident in one so young carried through to Hunuman's adulthod as, in what is a familiar story for so many former indentured labourers, he made a success of his life once freed from his contract, and ensured the lives of the generations that would follow him would be better than his own.

"He was illiterate, but he was a very smart guy," says Bharrath. "He came to work on the sugar plantations of Caroni Ltd. It was very hard labour, but better treatment than the African slaves. Eventually my grandfather became a foreman in the company and moved to work in the factory itself at Woodford Lodge.

"After his contract finished, he moved into agriculture and established himself in the village [Edinburgh Village (formerly Chase Village) in Chaguanas]. He educated those he could educate, he married my grandmother, who was born here, in an arranged wedding and had nine children. My grandfather did agriculture until the day he died. He sold eggplant to send one of his sons to school, and this son became a prominent doctor. He is still known as the 'Baigan [eggplant] Doctor'."

But while the Ramoutar family – now in its fifth generation in Trinidad – became a success, this is entirely due to how Hunuman set things up for himself, and the hard work and enterprise of his children and grandchildren that followed. There has been no involvement from ancestors in India, and virtually no contact with them anyway – inevitably, since Hunuman would have had no idea what had happened to the parents and other relatives he had literally walked away from. Still, Bharrath says some people in India claimed to have known his grandfather, though he doubts this could possibly be true, and is suspicious of their motives.

"In the late '80s and early '90s, a group of Trinidadians became aware of their roots in Bihar and around that area and did a lot of research," he says. "A lot of them went back to India, looking for their ancestors, to find the family they came from. But I personally dispute [the reality of] this, because after 150 years, how could you know who is who?

"People in rural areas like Bihar would have been very poor, especially back then, so I think they were just looking to see what they could get. My uncle, Dr Ramoutar – the Baigan Doctor – went back, and everybody in the village said they knew my grandfather. How could they? He was just a boy when he left, 80 years before! They knew we [Indo-Trinidadians] would have been a lot better off than a lot of people in India at that point, so I think they fabricated stories to get money and stuff. They just wanted to get something from people from Trinidad, so they made stories up."

Bharrath, a martial arts coach and promoter, has himself been to India, albeit not in search of ancestors who he suspects would not be genuine. He travelled to Delhi in 2019 for work and, though his trip had nothing to do with indenture, it still offered a reminder of the persisting divide between Indians and Indo-Caribbeans, and the lack of awareness of indenture that exists in India.

"In the countryside, where most of the indentured labourers came from, they are more aware of it, I think, but in the city, I don't think they are," he says. "Most people were surprised to learn I am an Indian descendant. They've only seen Indo-Caribbeans through cricket and music and think there's only a few of us." (Trinidad's population is, in fact, 35.4 per cent Indian, outnumbering black African descendants – 34.2 per cent – according to the 201 census.)

And even among those who do know the story behind how a significant number of Indians have for generations lived in the Caribbean, Bharrath feels there is precious little kinship.

"They don't think much of us," he says. "A little story from my experience: at one point we were working [in India] with a couple of guys who were speaking Hindi. An old guy with me asked me if I could understand Hindi; I said I can't. He said 'you know what they're saying? They're talking about you, saying "look at this slave".' They still refer to us as slaves."

And Bharrath says certain attitudes pervade among Indo-Caribbeans about each other, too.

"I'm a bit of a trailblazer as an Indian," he says. "In Western countries, it's unheard of for Indians to excel in sports, especially combat sports. We are seen as a docile people. But I've been trying to break barriers, and what's surprised me is that it's the Indians who have shunned us. When Ria [Ramnarine, a Trinidadian boxer of Indian descent who Bharrath trained] won, it was like we didn't belong. Other Indians told us we shouldn't be doing these things.

"My son, Jason Ramoutar, became a champion kickboxer. You see, my name is a very Indian name, Bharrath, but my children take western names, because sometimes you're judged by your name."

As for why there is a divide between Indians and Indo-Caribbeans, or why Indo-Caribbeans in his experience prefer to "stay in their lane", Bharrath says it is "to a point" a legacy of indenture. He is not sure if there was a deliberate attempt by the colonial powers to sever ties between indentured Indians and their homeland relatives - "we just didn't have proper communication back then" - but the very nature of the programme meant a return wasn't feasible for the majority anyway.

In Hunuman's case, he had arrived in Trinidad on his own as a pre-teenage boy and then grew into adulthood while working on Caroni's plantations and factories. In that whole time, going from boy to man, and all that entails, he went without having any correspondence whatsoever with his parents or anyone else back home. Even if this was a result of circumstance rather than choice, he had made his life in Trinidad. "He probably wouldn't even have known his family or remembered anything if he went back," says Bharrath.

But he certainly believes there was intent to foster divisions between Indians and the African ex-slaves. "It was divide and conquer," he says. "If both sides view each other with suspicion, there is less chance of them working together to revolt."

This divide continues to this day in Trinidad, with politics and business essentially split along racial lines. "Indenture is partly to blame for this, yes, to a point," says Bharrath. "In politics there are a lot of factors. The other part is that in the early '70s we had a Prime Minister, Dr Eric Williams, who brought a lot of slave descendants to the country from Grenada. They were brought in to support the black-led parties and were taught from a very early age to be suspicious of us, and the Indians responded in kind.

"Before then, the people lived in harmony, especially the rural people. Rural blacks got on very fine with Indian people. My best friend growing up was black and we are still good friends today."

A positive outcome of indenture has undoubtedly been how the influx of Indians spurred development in the countries they were taken to. This is as true in Trinidad as elsewhere, but while some countries celebrate this, Bharrath says it can be a source of ethnic tension there.

"The development has been phenomenal, and the service and clerical sector is mostly Indian people," he says. "But some people resent that. If you look at it unbiased, there's been a lot of positive contributions to the country [from Indians] – but they think we are taking something from them instead."

LIFE STORIES:
STUCK IN THE PAST
By curtsey of Oliver Fennell

The indentured labourers of India were taken to the Caribbean more than a century and a half ago, but the system's effects are not a thing of the past. Some descendants of the indentured continue to suffer, even if they know very little about what had preceded them in their family trees.

Joseph Mowlah-Baksh admits he doesn't know about his grandfather's journey from India to Trinidad. He doesn't even know where in India his grandfather came from. What he does know is that for most of his own life he has been stranded in a country other than the land of his birth, and the land to which he has always yearned to return. But not only has Joseph been unable to go back to Trinidad, he has been unable to travel anywhere since he his parents settled, with him and his four siblings, in Birmingham in 1972. Worse still, for more than 20 years now, he has been unable to work, having been rendered essentially stateless by a bureaucratic snafu caused by incomplete paperwork dating all the way back to his birth, in Trinidad, in 1958.

Now, at 66, Joseph has conceded that his working days are over. The red tape has finally been untangled, but it has come too late. A decade and a half without purpose has exacted a toll on his mental wellbeing, and in turn his physical health has suffered, as alcoholism filled the void once occupied by employment, and "15 years just sat on my arse with no social interaction" reduced his strength and mobility.

Still, there may yet be another chapter in Joseph's life. At the time of writing, he had just received his first passport, as well as his certificate of British citizenship. In a rare moment of levity in what is generally a sombre afternoon spent in his humble council house in a Birmingham suburb, Joseph jumps up from his couch, grinning, and asks: "Do you want to see it?, before retreating, literally rubbing his hands with pride, to his kitchen to retrieve a box containing all his important documents and extracting the pristine certificate that finally, officially, confirms that this man, who has spent 60 of his 66 years in Britain, and who was born to a British father and Irish mother, is, indeed, British.

"That's going in a frame," he says, beaming.

And what of his passport? That will surely be put to better use than serving as a piece of décor? But just because Joseph is now able to travel, it's not quite so straightforward – emotionally, at least.

"I wouldn't have a clue how to do it," he says. "Somebody would have to organise it for me and go with me. Even then, I have a lot of anxiety. My sister has a big house in Spain and she has invited me there, but I told her I'm not ready. I'll have to psyche myself up first. Or maybe she and her husband will have to kidnap me in the middle of the night and bundle me into a car to the airport!"

He can joke about it now, and whether or not Joseph does eventually travel again, at least he now has a choice. But there is an undeniable sadness about a man who was born far away, who then went back and forth between there and the UK before he finished high school, who sought ways to get back to Trinidad, who applied to work overseas, who dreamed of foreign holidays, now feeling wary of the wider world – or even much of the world beyond his own neighbourhood.

"I don't bother anyone," he says. "I just stay home with my budgies, YouTube and the radio. I go down to the local shops to pay my bills and get a couple of beers. My daughter tries to get me to go to the supermarket, but I don't fancy that."

It's a far cry from what he describes of his younger years in Trinidad, where he frolicked in the sea that lapped at his back garden, climbed trees and played outdoor sports; and when, in earlier adulthood in Birmingham he enjoyed the camaraderie of working in factories and on construction sites, and later took pride in a city centre department store job.

How did it come to this? How did a life, born of multiculturalism and with all the prospects that come with that, descend into one of humdrum routine, to the extent that a couple of beers and the company of budgies is a highlight?

To understand this, we have to go back to the beginning, to when Joseph Mowlah-Baksh was born in San Fernando on October 25, 1958. How Joseph came to be, and where he was born, was a result of his grandfather being an indentured worker, but it was the fact of Joseph's birth, in a foreign land with unfortunate timing, that caused him the bureaucratic nightmares he has fought his whole adult life.

"My grandfather went from India to Trinidad," he begins. "I'm afraid I don't know much about him. My father was the youngest of seven children, and I was the fourth of five, so my grandfather was already dead by the time I was born. As for his life, it just wasn't something I ever needed to know as a boy. Family in Trinidad would know more, but I've been unable to go back there, and most of the relatives I knew there have now passed away. The only memento I have of my grandparents is a photo of them, with him dressed in a very Victorian style, in a suit with a stud in the collar. She [his grandmother] was Indian too; darker than me. They met in Trinidad, but I don't know how.

"My father was born in Trinidad in August 1919. He was handsome; like an Asian Errol Flynn. No wonder my mum pulled him!"

Joseph's parents met in Birmingham, however. His dad, Andrew Mowlah-Baksh, had been a clerical worker in Trinidad before joining Britain's Royal Air Force, also in a clerical role, as Trinidad was a British colony at the time. Joseph's mother, Kathleen, originally from Ireland, was working as a patrol person with the military police and, after seeing this handsome "Asian Errol Flynn" around, she eventually made the first move and struck up a conversation. "And that's where I came from!" laughs Joseph.

They would marry and have their first three children in Birmingham, before Andrew decided to go home to Trinidad, taking the family with him - including Kathleen, who was pregnant with Joseph. But almost no sooner had they arrived than circumstances dictated a swift U-turn. A few months after their move, and shortly after Joseph's birth, Kathleen's mother fell seriously ill with TB, meaning Kathleen would have to go back to the UK to tend to her. She couldn't leave her four kids behind with Andrew, so the whole family headed straight back across the Atlantic when Joseph was nine months old.

These hectic developments, the sense of urgency surrounding them, and the worry that no doubt cloaked them, offer some complexion as to why an oversight was made when it came to Joseph's birth – one that would come to complicate his life so badly years later.

"My birth certificate was just a handwritten entry; a registration that a child was born," says Joseph. "I hadn't been named yet, but the birth had to be registered, so it just said 'a boy'."

Joseph produces this document. It is just as he says, but back in the '60s this was sufficient for the purposes of travel back to the UK, as babies and even children up to the age of 16 could simply be added to their parents' passports. Without any of the security measure of modern travel documents, Andrew and Kathleen Mowlah-Baksh used one family passport – still in Joseph's possession today – with the parents' photos simply glued in place and the names of their children handwritten on one page, including Joseph's squeezed in below those of his three older siblings. He is named here as "Abraham M. Baksh", after what would later be settled on as his middle name. Consequently, it was useless as identification for the person who would come to be called Joseph Mowlah-Baksh. Almost as useless as the birth certificate of "a boy".

Still, the family made it back to the UK and set up life there once again. After the hurried about-face and with the worry about Kathleen's mother's health, it is likely the parents simply forgot to finalise the paperwork for the newest child, and as the years past, and Joseph started attending school with no questions asked, and one more child followed, it simply never occurred to them that anything else would be needed – especially as they again returned to Trinidad when Joseph reached high school age.

"Dad had a house here [in Birmingham], but was missing home," says Joseph. "His older brother, Lance, came over with him [to the UK], because he served in the RAF as well, and they'd both been sending money home to pay for a house in Trinidad. So, Dad wanted to go back to take care of the house and their parents' affairs [after they died]. It was a beautiful white bungalow in Vistabella in San Fernando – you just walked out of the back garden and there was the sea.

"I went back at the right age. I was an adventurous lad, playing football, cricket in the street, climbing trees. It was all enlightening; an experience. I finished school at 14 and had a job sorted out on an oil rig, but suddenly we all came back to the UK because of some kind of falling-out in the family.

"I left behind all my friends and family and everything I'd learned, all the fun, at a time I was still finding our new stuff. But I thought I'd get a job, but when I came back to the UK, I found I had to do another school year!

"I finished school here and started working two weeks later, as a general machinist, operating drills, presses and assembly lines in a factory. I had a National Insurance number, so it was no problem. But I looked into going back [to Trinidad]. I was just a young lad and all my friends were there. I didn't have money for the fare, so I looked into the merchant navy, or working my passage, but I was too young."

Joseph therefore had to stay put – but he wouldn't have been able to leave anyway – not that he knew it at the time. He pressed on with work, got married and had children, but when his marriage failed, his thoughts turned to Trinidad again, and he found divorce was only the beginning of a series of problems that would dog him ever since.

"My next job was for more money, as a warehouse person in Habitat [department store] in the city centre; a rather prestigious place at the time," he says. "I met my wife just prior to that and we got married in 1977, had a son that same year and a daughter in 1980.

"We split up in 1982 and I was living on my own. I hadn't got a clue what to do with myself, so I thought I'd go back to Trinidad, get a job on the oil rig, sort out my parents' house, but I found out I couldn't get a passport.

"I'd done the application and was just waiting for the passport to come back, and they started running me in circles. They wanted more information, said I hadn't got the right pieces of paper, so I went down to London, to the West Indian High Commission, and explained my circumstances. Nearly every question they asked, I had nothing – all my paperwork was in Trinidad, but without a passport I couldn't go there, and if I couldn't go there, I couldn't get what I needed for a passport.

"So, I tried for an Irish one, since my mum was Irish. I went to the Irish centre in Digbeth [in Birmingham] and chatted about my background with a lovely old Irish lady. I brought all the papers and she started doing the form. Then she suddenly stopped and said 'Joseph, I can't help you – you've got no name!'

"That was when I first realised my birth certificate just said 'a boy'."

This left Joseph with no way to get to Trinidad – or anywhere else. He says he was offered a job in Italy that he was unable to take, and that when his friends invited him on holidays, the closest he'd get was driving them to the airport.

At least he had a driving licence. This proved invaluable not only for domestic travel, but for work too, when immigration laws regarding foreign workers were tightened up later in the 1980s – not that Joseph was foreign; he just couldn't get a British passport. But, for now at least, his driving licence was suitable for ID purposes.

"The laws got more serious; you had to prove you're eligible to work," he says. "If an employer employed somebody who wasn't entitled to work here, they'd get done for thousands of pounds. It had never been an issue for me, as I applied for jobs with my NI number as I always did. Then they asked for a passport or driving licence for ID as well, so I showed them my driving licence."

But in 1998, the UK government started phasing in plastic driving licences with photo ID to replace the old paper ones which didn't carry any images. When Joseph came to replace his in 2000, his situation worsened still.

"I went to change my driving licence from paper to plastic and the place of birth flagged up with a red ring around Trinidad," he says. "The guy handling my application said it's not a problem, just put your passport number on the form…"

Which, of course, Joseph could not do. Now he was left without a passport or a driving licence.

"The last couple of jobs I went for, from the interview I'd got the job, they shook my hand, said thank you and 'when you come to start work, can you bring your passport or driving licence for ID?'. I had to say sorry, I don't have either, and they had to withdraw the job offer.

"I'd worked my whole life, until the driving licence changed, and now I was on benefits. I could still get them with my NI number, but with no work I was left just sat on my arse with no social interaction. I'm patient and I can work hard, but I got so bored, and then anxiety and physical problems set in.

"This situation nicked a piece of me; it hit my confidence. I did class myself as an alcoholic at one point. My routine was to watch the 9 o'clock film and open a bottle of wine, but the next day I usually couldn't remember it. I'd find trays of Chinese takeaway that I couldn't remember ordering. I've fallen in the bath and down the stairs a few times and hurt my back. One time I woke up next to a pool of blood and I had no idea what had happened.

"I sought counselling and they told me to keep drinks diaries. I got to 50 years old [in 2008] and told myself 'right, I've got 15 years [of working life] left, I've got to sort myself out. I attended courses while I was unemployed and took voluntary work. Voluntary work was my saviour – all the clothes I wear, the furnishings you see here, they came from charity shops I worked in."

Joseph never did make a return to paid-for employment, as his anxiety worsened and his physical condition deteriorated, and now he is at retirement age anyway. His efforts to "sort myself out" were not entirely in vain, though, because he is now indeed the proud owner of a British passport and citizenship certificate.

And if Joseph's problems have, in a sense, been a knock-on effect of his grandfather's history as an indentured worker, that same thing was what led to their belated resolution. Specifically, the Windrush scandal of recent years was what brought Joseph's plight to the attention of some influential media professionals. It turns out his father was a passenger on the Empire Windrush's maiden voyage in 1948 when he first moved to the UK from Trinidad, and while Andrew himself never faced any immigration issues, Joseph's case as his offspring has been deemed worthy of compensation.

"There was a professor who was compiling a book about Windrush; he was looking at the Windrush manifest," he says. "Then *The Guardian* got in touch with me after going through his list, seeing my father's name and then working out I was his son."

Guardian journalist Amelia Gentleman contacted Joseph initially for information about his father as part of a story marking the 75th anniversary of the Windrush's first sailing, but soon uncovered Joseph's own unfortunate tale. This was published in the newspaper in April 2023, which in turn attracted the attentions of ITV.

"My granddaughter saw me in *The Guardian* and came to show me and said 'Look, Grandpa, you're famous!'," Joseph says. "Then ITV read it and I got involved with that. They came and did three days of filming here [in the house]. Now I've got my bits, they want to come back and do a final sequence, and then put a documentary out."

Joseph "got his bits" thanks to Amelia Gentleman and the ITV crew encouraging him to give one more push to get his paperwork sorted, with their help. "We accumulated all the stuff and went for the passport again," he says. "We gave them everything; my parents' passports, every single piece of paper I could think of. There was nothing else I could give them – if they didn't have it, I didn't have it.

"They accepted it, then I went and did my biometrics, and just like that, it [the passport] arrived! A couple of days before that, my citizenship certificate had arrived.

"It was because of *The Guardian* the wheels were set in motion. They helped in the background, as did ITV. I said to Amelia 'thank you – in four months, you have sorted out what's taken 40 years.'"

Now, with all his documents in order, if Joseph can overcome the anxiety he feels about finally travelling again, he has some big ideas about what he wants to do – especially with the prospect of reparation in sight.

"I'm just waiting now," he says of the outcome of his application to the Windrush Compensation Scheme. "There's no more involvement from me; it's all in their hands. I don't know how much I'll get, but they're considering loss of earnings, which they can calculate, and mental torment – but how do you put a price on that?

"A good thing about my situation is it has got me back in touch with my sisters and brothers. We didn't have a central thing without our parents, but my family knew I had these issues and have helped me. I'm not promising anything until I get the funds, which is down to the Windrush side of things, but I'd like to book a cruise for all the family and just go everywhere, see the whole lot, rent a deck for everybody. Even if we get sick of each other, we can hang off and look at the sea like I did when I was a boy going to Trinidad."

And might Joseph finally make it back to Trinidad?

"If I went back now, there would only be a few cousins left," he says of the family there. "I see them on Facebook; they've all got grown-up families. Everyone else has died. If I'd had a passport, I could have seen them when they were alive.

"My dad's brother went back, and he died within a week or so of arriving. I like to think he had a calling. Maybe I do too. I'd definitely like to go back. I look at places there on YouTube, the streets from when I was growing up, and see how they've changed, but I want to see it for myself. I'm sick of seeing things on the TV.

"I've been nowhere since 1972; done nothing. I think of all the things I could have done; the things I haven't learned as an adult.

"I haven't had a good memory for a long, long while. I've just want to see something nice before I die."

LIFE STORIES:
A TALE OF TRIUMPH
By curtsey of Oliver Fennell

Not that they knew it, or each other, but the forebears of both Joe Mowlah-Baksh and Helen-Claire Tingling, a health board director based in Ontario, Canada, were on the Empire Windrush's first sailing to England. It was Joe's father, Andrew, who travelled from Trinidad to the UK as a young, single man who would later meet Joe's mother and begin the series of work, life and family events that would inadvertently leave his son in such a bind for such a long time. Meanwhile, on the same ship at the same time was Egbert Tingling, a man of Indian descent who was departing Jamaica, also as a young single man, for a new life in Britain. He would become the father of Helen-Claire, a woman whose life experience has played out very differently to Joe's, and who has rare insight into not only South Asian indenture but also African slavery, as her family tree stems from both branches.

While Joe's experience has been characterised by frustration and involuntary inaction, Helen-Claire's has been as multicultural as the woman herself, with spells in Jamaica and Wales preceding her current life in Canada. While Joe's imposed stagnation has bred in him anxiety and regret, Helen-Claire's rich life experiences have afforded her perspective and appreciation, not just for the opportunities she has enjoyed, but even for the fact of indenture having created those conditions for the generations that followed her great-grandfather.

As with so many current-day descendants of the indentured, Helen-Claire's knowledge of her ancestors prior to a certain point is minimal. As far as she can determine with confidence, the story starts with her great-grandfather, Jagh Mohan Sau (later known as John Tingling). However, it cannot be confirmed if he was born in Jamaica to parents who had made the journey from India, or if he made the journey himself when he was very young, alongside parents whose precise identities are essentially lost to the passing of time.

"I don't know when my paternal great-grandfather made the journey, or even if he did. Jagh Mohan Sau was born in 1849, which going by the timing of it fits the indenture period," says Helen-Claire. "I don't know when he arrived in Jamaica – it's possible he travelled as a child – or if he was born there."

It is believed the Tingling name was given to the Sau family by their employers when they arrived in Jamaica, as was common practice in indenture contracts. Similarly, it was also common for Indians to adopt western first names, thus Jagh Mohan became John.

However, and whenever, John came to be in Jamaica, it would in any case be his home and that of the descendants to follow, until his grandson – Helen Claire's father, Egbert – boarded Windrush on May 24, 1948.

"Growing up, my father [Egbert] talked to me about pleasant memories he had as a boy of his *aji* and *aja* [paternal grandparents] carrying him on their shoulders to harvest mushrooms," Helen-Claire continues. "The mushroom-gathering that my father remembered so fondly therefore must have been his grandparents' work. It would not have been unusual for children to have been in the fields at that time in history.

"His grandfather [John] died in Jamaica in 1929, when he was 80, and his listed occupation on the death certificate was 'labourer'. His grandmother died in 1932 and her listed occupation was 'cultivator'.

"It was just the language of the time, but it showed they were labourers. 'Coolie' was the word commonly used for indentured servants. This suggests to me that John and Sarah were already out of indentureship, but not yet landowners.

Helen-Claire is someone who, while well aware of the inherent abuses that created and facilitated indenture, sees a positive in such a regrettable part of history, or at least in what unfolded as a result of it. While not for one minute excusing those behind indenture, Helen-Claire would prefer to focus not on the negatives of what was endured but rather the positive eventual outcomes of many of the South Asians who made the journey across the *kalapani*. This, she says, is testament to something that should be celebrated – the resiliency of the human spirit – and that the rewards of this spirit were ultimately opportunities for multi-generational success.

"Of course, indentured servants did better than slaves, because they had less barriers against them," says Helen-Claire. "It was something they decided to do, and something they could choose to leave [once their contracts were finished]. It wasn't like the African slaves, who were kidnapped. No matter how one-sided the contracts were, or how bad the conditions and treatment turned out to be, they still had to agree to do it. The workers would have seen the move to Jamaica as a means to make better lives for themselves, and many of them had resources. As a result, many were able to move on with their own lives after the initial period of indenture. Today, we might refer to these workers as entrepreneurs.

"Bear in mind the kind of character that decided 'let's go and try that in another country' – they had to have had an entrepreneurial streak in the first place to even try that, and that explains why many of them triumphed."

It is Helen-Claire's contention that an inherent entrepreneurial spirit in many of the indentured workers, which spurred them to make that initial journey – regardless of any subterfuge in recruitment or any abuses that followed – is what helped many of them succeed in these foreign lands once their contracts ended. Her belief is perhaps affirmed by the high incidence in the region of South Asian business owners, merchants and white-collar professionals.

In her family's case, she says, "in a relatively short time, they managed to do OK for themselves – they went from indentured to land ownership in 100 years, setting up businesses".

"Indian indentured workers often quickly transitioned out of indentureship. This is the reason Jamaica started to import workers from China in 1860. John had the means to get out of indenture after one term. Subsequently, Wilfred [John's son/Egbert's father] became a landowner. The story is therefore one of prosperity – from indenture to landowner within only two generations. After he married my grandmother, Jimima Jackson, Wilfred bought Beckford Lodge. I understand that the Jacksons were wealthy, and the combined Jackson-Tingling resources likely made the purchase possible. As well as this, Wilfred also became a tailor and a Baptist preacher.

"Beckford Lodge was part of the extensive holdings of the Beckford Family. They were of British high society and became part of Jamaican society also. It was on Dalling Street in Sav-la-Mar, in Westmoreland, Jamaica; and a part of it was severed from the larger Beckford-owned parcel and purchased by my ancestors.

"Under Tingling ownership, Beckford Lodge was a farm with cattle and chickens. The acreage also had fruit trees and a pond. Part of the acreage held a dry goods store. The property was sold after my grandmother's death in 2009. The Beckford name lives on in Sav-la-Mar and across the whole island, adorning numerous streets and buildings."

Meanwhile, Helen-Claire says her maternal ancestors – descendants of African slaves – showed similar spirit: "I'm proud to know that both sides of my family triumphed over their circumstances of slavery and indenture. My mother's father, Zachariah Byfield, came from the slave side, but remarkably on both sides of the family they did OK. It was a similar story, this time within 60 years. It's likely that it was Zachariah's grandfather – my great-great-grandfather – who transitioned out of slavery. Zachariah was born in 1893 – 45 years after slavery was abolished in 1838. That's two generations.

"Slaves were moved out of slavery into apprenticeship from 1834. More than one thousand slaves were able to buy out their freedom within two years. I believe that my great-great-grandfather was amongst the first group that transitioned out of slavery, and my great-grandfather who established the farm. I understand it was a crop farm.

"He [Zachariah] ran away when he was twelve. He stowed away on a ship sailing out of Port Antonio to Bristol. He was the eldest child and the other three were girls, so he was a beast of burden. Life was bad in Jamaica, working the farm with his father, so off he took.

"He went to Bristol, worked on ships for a bit, and joined an Italian circus travelling through Europe. I believe that Zach had an operational or maintenance job with the circus. That was when they used to exhibit 'darkies' and the hugely obese and people with physical disabilities, gays and lesbians – all were considered 'freaks', quote-unquote. Due to this societal view, he – a black man -- was able to find a place in that community. He arrived in Barry [in Wales] in 1919 and eventually became the manager of The Colonial Club there. It was a place for coloured servicepeople. I don't like that term, 'coloured', but that's how it was back then. Zach met my grandmother [Margaret] in Barry."

Zachariah and Margaret would marry and have children, one of which would be Helen-Claire's mother, Icilda, who grew up with The Colonial Club and would meet and marry Egbert, a customer at the Club, shortly after he too alighted in Barry following an escape from an overbearing situation back in Jamaica.

"My father's story is similar to that of my maternal grandfather," says Helen-Claire. "He had an argument with his father. There were 14 children and my dad was the oldest son. Children were still chattel back then, and treated as such.

"My father went to Manning's prep school [in Westmoreland] but he also had farm chores at Beckford Lodge. Life was hard in Jamaica at that time, and my father told me that he often went to bed hungry. My dad told me that if he got in trouble at school, he would be caned by the headmaster and punished again by his father when he got home.

"My father found his father tough to work with as the head of the household, so he left to join the Armed Forces. He enlisted into the RAF when he was 17 and was part of the second contingent of volunteers. I understand that he received training under the Royal Canadian Air Force banner, as part of the British Commonwealth Air Training Plan.

"Jamaica was still a British colony, so as a British citizen he was eligible to work in the UK, and when was demobbed after the War he was offered training in broadcasting, as he had done some broadcasting for the Forces. That's what he was doing in Wales; he went there to pick up work as a broadcaster. He'd gone home after the War, but it hadn't worked out. There wasn't much going on in Jamaica for young men. He went to Britain to follow what he thought were his fortunes, to take the professional training that was offered to all British veterans. He became a radio engineer and subsequently got a broadcasting job in Barry.

"He was on the very first Windrush sailing; he landed on June 22, 1948. He was on there as part of the contingent of British servicemen who would be offered work. Lots of people on that had overcome tremendous difficulties and went on to achieve amazing things.

"My parents met at The Colonial Club in Barry where Zachariah Byfield was the manager. My mother had a child during the War, so there was an instant family when they began married life in December 1948. They raised ten children together across a wide age range.

"The broadcasting work dried up. They offered to transfer my father, and it would have been a promotion, but he couldn't take his wife and children, so he said no. The next few years were very difficult, as he tried to get job after job. He wasn't proud; he would do anything. But he'd got the broadcasting work because he had this wonderful voice that didn't betray his origins. People didn't realise, speaking over the phone, that he wasn't white. He'd get an interview [for a job], travel to it, and then when they saw the colour of his skin, he'd be told to push off.

"He ended up doing a lot of menial jobs and bought a house with no indoor plumbing or heating; a typical post-War British home. Looking back, there was nothing he couldn't do. He would do his job, have his dinner, then put on his overalls and knock down a wall or put in some plumbing. He welded, he painted, he put in windows, and he lay cement. My father did many self-improvements, figuring it out as he went along. He always fixed his own cars. I grew up believing he could do anything, Related to indenture, 'work hard' was one of the tenets my father gave to me: 'You can't give up, you have to persevere, and you can do anything'.

"He also taught me the benefits of multiculturalism and not to dislike people based on their ethnicity or national origin. He was like the United Nations – he welcomed everybody! So, I always look for the good in people. I don't want to look at one slice of history [indenture] and say 'those awful white people did these awful things to us' – it wasn't because they were white or even that they were awful. It's just that's what life was like back then. And I think a good way to look at adverse circumstances is to ask yourself: 'What is it that I'm meant to get from this?'

"So, in terms of indenture, while it's important we recognise what happened, I believe it's also important not to dwell on it, and to look forward instead. My father also told me, 'It's not where you come from, it's where you're going that matters.' He took pride in telling people he came from nothing and he believed the measure of success is doing your best with what you've been given. It was similar for my grandfather, who arrived in Jamaica with nothing and made a success of it.

"I see all this victimology going on, but I don't think my granddad was in an unusual situation. People left by choice, took their skills and believed they could do better. Those kinds of people would have succeeded regardless. They thought it was a good thing, or they wouldn't have done it. What they thought they could do, they did!

"One of the big lessons – one from a long list – that my father taught me, and which I have tried to pass on to my own children, is: 'Life isn't fair, but concentrate on what you have rather than what you don't have. Work hard and do the best with the hand you've been given.'

"When you see how well the Asians are doing [in the Caribbean], it really is a story of great triumph."

CONCLUSION

It was a sense of shame that propelled this book. I am ashamed that the country I live in could be responsible for the atrocity that was indentured labour. More importantly, I am ashamed that the country I came from facilitated it, and then largely buried it. But most importantly of all, I am ashamed of myself – that I was born in raised in Kolkata, one of the heartlands of indenture; a place from where thousands of my kin were taken; one of the key ports from which they were shipped to unknown lands, uncertain fates and certain misery, and yet I knew nothing about it. I had lived for 35 years in this city without ever realising its role in one of the darkest chapters in Indian and British history. At the same time, I possessed a view of Britain that was shared by many Indian people – that it was a place where people were nice, courteous, erudite and sophisticated. Through childhood, I read a lot about British arts and culture, and consumed the works of its great writers and poets, and I wanted to see for myself this place where I was led to believe everything – and everybody – was good. I wanted to see this land of my dreams.

This dream was realised in 1981 when I was sponsored by the Hotel and Catering Institutional Management Association (HCIMA) to take a course in

Poole, Dorset, that would qualify me to become a member of the association. I had already founded a hospitality institute in Guwahati, Assam, so this was the next step in my career. I would ultimately become a life fellow of the HCIMA, but my motivation for travelling to the UK was not for money or a good job – I wanted to immerse myself in the culture I had read so much about, and to interact with the people I held in such high esteem.

As was to be expected, the realities did not quite match the fantasy. Of course, there were plenty of nice people and a vast number of cultural attractions, but in any country you will come across good and bad. It's just that in India we never read or heard anything bad about Britain. Still, on balance, the positives outweighed the negatives. It may not have been the idyll portrayed by the wordsmiths I so loved, but there were greater opportunities to earn, to progress, and maybe even to settle. I got a work permit and I stayed, and while it was a struggle at times, as I did all kinds of odd jobs to make ends meet, I am happy with the choices I have made and the professional and personal life I have built. Moving to the UK widened my world and opened my eyes to a lot of things that I may never have known had I stayed in India.

One of these was indenture – but that wasn't until decades later. After securing my HCIMA qualifications and working in those aforementioned odd jobs, I moved to Wales – Caerphilly in South Wales, to be exact – where I managed care homes for the elderly. In a natural progression of this, I moved north to pursue a Master's degree in gerontology at Bangor University, graduating in 2006. I found Bangor to my liking and settled in North Wales, basing myself in Colwyn Bay where, in 2015-16 I would serve as mayor, but before that setting up a foundation that would finally open my eyes to indenture.

I opened a second-hand bookshop in the town, and from its office I launched NWAMI in 2011. This was initially the North Wales Association for Multicultural Integration, and later rebranded as Networking for World Awareness of Multicultural Integration as the group grew and took on more of an international approach and involvement. As somebody who both embodies and has prospered from multiculturalism, I wanted to further promote its importance, especially at a time when cultural divisions seem more acute than ever, and are even exploited for political gain. Divide and conquer has, after all, been a tried and tested strategy over the centuries, and perhaps never more so than during the period of indenture.

One year, during South Asian Heritage Month, which runs every July 18 to August 17 and is aimed at celebrating the roots of the South Asian diaspora wherever they may be, I was browsing related content on social media and I came across a discussion about slavery. A member of NWAMI was involved in the conversation and she asked: "Did you know about slavery for Indian people as well?"

To my shame, I did not – not as someone who hails from Kolkata, nor as someone who has lived, worked and studied internationally, nor even as someone who purportedly led a network with the precise remit of increasing knowledge about the people and cultures of the world. I started looking into this "slavery for Indian people". OK, it wasn't slavery in the strict definition of the word, but it was very similar – exploitative, abusive, racist, trading off social inequalities, dangerous and even, for some, deadly. My research into the subject had a snowball effect – the more I learned, the more I wanted to learn, and the pace this gathered was driven by my own emotions, which ranged from pity for my fellow South Asians who had suffered under indenture, to anger at the Indian and British people and institutions responsible for it, to my own sense of shame at being hitherto oblivious to all this and wanting to make amends by bringing the issue to the fore, opening doors and boxes that segments of Indian society in particular would rather keep firmly shut.

Once I started looking, I found the legacy of indenture everywhere. It is only India and Britain that seeks to downplay it, which is both as ironic as it is obvious. Many of the smaller countries and islands to where the indentured were taken fully acknowledge this key part of their histories and actively celebrate the contributions that South Asians have made to their cultures, economies and infrastructures. There are museums, commemorative days and events, cultural centres and academic departments delving into the subject, and while even in these countries there was for a long time little by way of serious study into indenture, people are now increasingly researching it, writing about it and, most importantly, talking about it. While this is gathering pace, particularly in the Caribbean, thankfully people are now becoming more aware of it in Britain, especially as a follow-on from the publicity generated by the Windrush scandal.

India, though, in many ways remains more difficult. There is a sense that many Indian people don't want to know about indenture even when they are told about it; that either they are ashamed some of their ancestors may have been indentured, or worse, that their ancestors may have facilitated indenture. It also plays into India's enduring culture of class and caste divide. The indentured were almost all from low caste, so latter-day middle-class Indians may not want to admit their ancestors were from a lesser demographic, or, hideously, may not care that these people suffered, simply because they were *dalit*.

The irony of such snobbery is, though, that the indentured Indians exhibited the very best traits of South Asian people – they were hard-working, savvy, entrepreneurial, adaptable and driven by a motivation to improve their lives and those of their families, both present and future. They deserve not just our sympathy but also our admiration. Yes, they were taken advantage of, but the key difference between slavery and indenture is that the workers themselves had to take the first step. Bear in mind they were often from the lowest strata of Indian society and, as such, condemned by the very same sentiments which continue to look down on them and their histories today to remain there. It was only by taking a chance on an opportunity elsewhere – as flawed as it was – that they had even a meagre chance at doing something better with their lives. No, they didn't really know where they were going, nor what they were signing up for; they just took a chance. And, while undeniably they suffered on the ships and on the plantations, and some did not even survive the journey or for the duration of their contracts, it did in the long run work out for many. This was not thanks to the exploitative forces that took them away, nor to the repulsive forces inside India that drove them out – it was in spite of them. We cannot thank those behind indenture for the "opportunity"; rather we thank those brave souls who made the journey, endured the torment, and then made a success of their new circumstances. They, the downtrodden in India, became the parents and grandparents of the professionals, academics and diplomats of the Caribbean today.

In that regard, the motivation behind this book and my efforts to bring indenture into the light is not to seek reparation for those who suffered. The current generation is not responsible for the sins of past ones. Compensation, or even contrition, is not what I'm calling for. Simple acknowledgement would be appreciated – acknowledgement of sacrifices and contributions made, of bravery, of spirit, and of efforts to preserve Indian culture and identity in faraway lands, at the same time as enriching the existing cultures and identities of those lands. To a great extent those host countries already do so, but I am calling on the Britain and particularly India to simply acknowledge the wrongdoings of past governments, and to not only recognise the legacy of the indentured, but to embrace it.

Beyond this, I am content to let bygones be bygones, and to move forward. Because that is exactly what the indentured did.

They moved forward.

FURTHER READING

Articles

"Protest Songs Of East Indians In British Guiana" by Ved Prakash Vatuk, *The Journal Of American Folklore*, Vol 77, No 305, The American Folklore Society (1964)

"Immobilising Labour: Regulation of Indentured Labour in Assam and the British West Indies, 1830-1926" by Prabhu P Mohapatra, Integrated Labour History Research Programme, VV Giri National Labour Institute (2004)

"The Brown Atlantic: Re-thinking Post-Slavery" by Devi Hardeen, University of Liverpool (2012)

Columns by Bridget Brereton in the *Daily Express* newspaper (www.trinidadexpress.com) from 2018 until now

"The Leonara Strike and Riots of 1939" (Parts One and Two) by Tota Mangar, *Guyana Chronicle*, February 14, 2022, and February 16, 2022

Books

Bechu: Bound Coolie Radical in British Guiana 1894-1901, Clem Seecharan, The University of the West Indies Press, 1999, ISBN-10 9766400717

The Blackest Thing In Slavery Was Not The Black Man, Eric Williams (edited by Brinsley Samaroo), The University of the West Indies Press, 2022, ISBN 9789766407476

Glimpses of the Sugar Industry : The Art of Garnet Ifill, Brinsley Samaroo, Hansib Publications, 2015, ISBN-10 1906190984

In Place of Slavery: A Social History of British Indian and Javanese Laborers in Suriname, Rosemarjin Hoefte, University Press of Florida, 1998, ISBN-10 0813016258

Literature of Girmitiya: History, Culture and Identity, edited by Neha Singh and Sajaudeen Chapparban, Springer Nature Singapore, 2023, ISBN 9789811946202

A New System of Slavery: Export of Indian Labour Overseas, 1830-1920, Hugh Tinker, Oxford University Press, 1974, ISBN 9780192184108

The Still Cry: Personal Accounts Of East Indians In Trinidad And Tobago During Indentureship, 1845-1917, Noor Kumar Mahabir, Cataloux Publications, 1985, ISBN-10 0911565035

A Question of Labour: Indentured Immigration into Trinidad & British Guiana, 1875-1917, KO Laurence, St Martin's Press, 1994, ISBN 9780312121723

www.ingramcontent.com/pod-product-compliance
Ingram Content Group UK Ltd.
Pitfield, Milton Keynes, MK11 3LW, UK
UKHW020727290425
457955UK00006B/32/J

9 781835 636831